Sacred Journey

Sacred Journey

a Companion *for* Rudolf Schwarz's
The Church Incarnate

GERALD ROBINSON

Wipf & Stock · Eugene, Oregon

SACRED JOURNEY

a Companion for Rudolf Schwarz's "The Church Incarnate."

Copyright © 2020 Gerald Robinson. All rights reserved. Except for brief quotations in critical publications or reviews no part of this book may be reproduced in any manner without prior written permission from the publisher. Write: Permissions, Wipf and Stock Publishers, 199 W. 8th Avenue, Suite 3, Eugene, OR 97401.

Wipf and Stock
An Imprint of Wipf and Stock Publishers
199 W. 8th Ave., Suite 3,
Eugene, OR 97401

www.wipfandstock.com

PAPERBACK ISBN: 978-1-5326-9898-9
HARDCOVER ISBN: 978-1-5326-9899-6
EBOOK ISBN: 978-1-5326-9900-9

Manufactured in the U.S.A.

Some of the material in this work also appears in *Rebuilding the Church on a New Foundation*, published concurrently by Wipf and Stock.

Cover:
interior of St. Fronleichnam Church in Aachen, Germany, 1928.
Rudolf Schwarz, Architect.
see page 60.

Contents

	Foreword to the German Edition	ix
I	THE FOUNDATION	1
II	THE FIRST SIX PLANS	22
	The First Plan *for the Ministry of Contemplation* . . .	31
	The Second Plan *for the Ministry of Pastoral Care* . . .	36
	The Third Plan *for the Ministry of Witness*	46
	The Fourth Plan *for the Ministry of Dedication*	55
	The Fifth Plan *for the Ministry of Evangelism*	66
	The Sixth Plan *for the Ministry of Justice*	72
III	THE SEVENTH? PLAN	76
IV	THE TEST	84
	Epilogue	117
	Bibliography	118
	Photo Credits	119
	Index	120

Romano Guardini's Foreword to the 1938 German edition of Rudolf Schwarz's "The Church Incarnate."
Translation: Gerald Robinson

With this foreword I would like to do more than just say that the book that follows is important, because I feel this book requires an introduction. The book comes from a new starting point and has an unfamiliar way of seeing things. Its thoughts are interwoven in many ways, flowing in deep streams, so it's not easy to read. Now I could be wrong. Perhaps it will seem familiar and liberating to some who have been waiting for years for such a work to appear. Others, however, will find it dark and difficult, but they too should read it.

This is a book about which one could easily write a much larger book; in fact it's more a topic than a book: a group of themes full of light and potential, so I see my role as pointing out their significance. This may serve the reader as a set of instructions for the use of the book: instructions to be set aside once he commences reading.

Above all, I noticed something hardly to be expected in a volume about church construction: its strangely intense approach to the human image. This is an attempt to discover in the proportions of the human body a connection between the body and the world by saying, for example, that man is that being which has a hand. This human image is very concrete and exists through all areas of being from the material to the heights of the mind, even a mind infused with the holy spirit. In determining the form of the human being the essence of the world is also named—for every real human form is a broad image—and out of each rises a wonderfully vital overall form of existence. In order to reach this point the author has had to put aside what is generally assumed about man and his world, but you should follow him with confidence because he sees with clear eyes and feels with a warm heart.

This way of being arises from a true encounter with reality. The artist, above all, is aware of this connection; but many a thinker, philosopher or theologian could also be open to such a possibility; a possibility which he could not find within his own discipline. The book could also be welcomed by any person who finds it comfortable to live in such a reality. It seems to me that it should be possible to translate the deep thoughts of this writing into a very simple language; I'm sure there are many who would wish this to be true.

Furthermore, this book embraces a very primitive consciousness of what we call a church. Even the illustrations of churches are not based on concepts of construction but of a living happening. "Church" here is presented as a process, a process passing through world-time. This is a very dynamic picture which does not deny the conventional view of the church but wonderfully complements it. The reader also feels how the local community which is present in celebrations of the Holy Mysteries is constantly condensing from that great event; but this gathering to which we belong every Sunday receives from such a context a wonderful world.

The third thing that I felt when reading this book is not easy to express. I wondered where I had ever experienced the mental or spiritual flow that it embodies. Where does it spring from, what is its provenance? At first there seemed to be a connection to the small forgotten writings of the historical Gethsemane by Konrad Weiss, but going further back; for instance to Paracelsus, to Eckhart, to the hymns of Notker and to the world of early Nordic Christianity. These would be promising connections, the character and meaning of which would not be easy to grasp—one would then have to write that second book of which there has been much discussion.

Out of these connections architectural problems arise. The architectural forms of church appear as great interfaces between man and his world, between human history and divine action; as clarifications of that mysterious procession in which the people of God travel through time; as huge symbols on which the Christian being can be seen in time, and as the liturgies in which it takes place.

I have said a lot about this book, but I hope not too much. I am used to being criticized—one is often criticized over details without the total experience being appreciated, and if total clarity were demanded one could hardly publish anything. Newly created connections cannot be presented in full clarity immediately, and time must be allowed for discussions about the extent of the possible. In any case, the book is not only worth reading, but offers itself as a valuable source for meditation. It will be a great force for the interpretation of divine order.

ROMANO GUARDINI
Berlin, 1938

PART I
The Foundation

Beginning the Journey

Rudolf Schwarz, a German architect and mystic, is famous for designing some beautiful churches, but he is more renowned for his 1938 work[1] *Vom Bau der Kirche* (from Building to Church.) In that work he proposed a system of ideas, what he called "The Six Plans" that would embrace all the worship of the Christian Church. It was extraordinary that Schwarz could record these tender insights into prayer and adoration at a time when Germany was entering its darkest hour. The nation around him was being led by dark forces and entranced by manic visions of a destiny for its blood. Fear was being institutionalized, and religious rituals were being subverted to the glorification of the state and for an eternity that was to last for a millennium.

FIGURE 1. Rudolf Schwarz 1897–1961

It was extraordinary that in this hate-filled environment Schwarz could conduct his gentle inquiry into forms and spaces of worship. After surviving the devastation of his nation and the deaths of its leaders it was even more extraordinary that he would be made responsible for the planning and rebuilding of the central area of the city of Cologne, a task for which he was

---

1. Schwarz, Rudolf. *Vom Bau der Kirche*. Heidelberg: Verlag Lambert Schneider, 1938.

entrusted as he was one of the few German architects who had not been associated with the previous Nazi regime.

Twenty years later, in 1958, an English translation[2] by Cynthia Harris of Schwarz's book titled *The Church Incarnate* with a foreword by Mies van der Rohe was published. The Canadian Architect magazine received a review copy, and the editor, John Kettle, invited me to write the review. I had just arrived in Canada after graduating with a Master of Architecture degree from the Urban Design Studio at Harvard, but my real background was as a structural engineer which perhaps explains why I found the book so incredibly difficult to read. Its repetitive poetic style and elliptical imagery would send me to sleep, its undulating prose a lullaby, so at the end of a page I would have no memory of what I had just read. At the same time, perhaps because it was so foreign to me, I felt there was something of real value in the book, something just out of reach. I phoned John Kettle to say I needed more time. I needed a lot more time—several years in fact. By the time I was able to write the review the book was out of print! It took me ten years to be able to read Schwarz's book, taking it a little at a time. It took another ten years to be able to put it to use, and a further ten years for me to be able to teach it.

There is general agreement that the work is difficult. In his preface to the German edition (I've attached my translation as a Foreword) Fr. Romano Guardini, a friend of Schwarz, wrote[3] "The book comes from a new starting point and has an unfamiliar way of seeing things. Its thoughts are interwoven in many ways, flowing in deep streams, so it's not easy to read." These sentiments were echoed in the English edition, both in the Foreword by Mies van der Rohe and the Translator's Invitation by Cynthia Harris.

From a superficial reading of the "Contents" page many have assumed that after an introductory chapter the book examines six church plans, finds them all wanting, then proceeds to a seventh plan which tests out. Nothing could be further from the truth. Schwarz's sacred journey is not a straight line; it is a combination of a maze and a labyrinth. A maze because it opens up all sorts of seductive avenues which turn out to be dead ends; and a

---

2. Schwarz, Rudolf. *The Church Incarnate,* Translated by Cynthia Harris. Chicago: Henry Regnery, 1958.

3. Guardini, Zum Geleit: *Vom Bau der Kirche.*

labyrinth because its value lies not in its inevitable conclusion but in the insights gained along the way. Schwarz chose not to eliminate from his prose those non-essential decorations which he carefully excised from his architecture. It brings to mind a quotation[4] by Paul Claudel: "the parts that you don't understand, they are the most beautiful of all!"

Cynthia Harris's translation of Schwarz's work has been my companion for sixty years. For sixty years I have enjoyed her beautiful evocative prose that reads like poetry yet remains true to the original. My reverence for this book does not mean I understand it; in fact I don't believe that such a thing could be possible. To understand means to perceive a meaning in something, but Schwarz's words change their meanings from sentence to sentence. He dwells in a spiritual dimension where he was able to see qualities beyond those of our physical world. Sometimes he is worldly, and sometimes he is God-centered. In that world words may have multiple meanings, and opposites are free to co-exist, so in his writings: that which is open may also be perceived as closed, dark may be light, clear may be opaque, space may become an object, and all directions may be reversed. All this can create confusion. In his world one has to surrender to the moment and avoid importing the logic of the physical world into the spiritual. For an example of this layering of meanings we could look at his illustrations of a curved wall (figures 2 and 3) which is a barrier between inside and outside, but also may be the reflector of a searchlight sending a beam of light into heavens, or a telescope focusing on a distant star, so it could either project or receive light.

A further layering lies in his title for this formation. He calls this light-filled space "The Dark Chalice," possibly to indicate the process by which the space empties itself of light and thus creates darkness.

In another version the wall itself could be dematerialized, becoming a pathway along which the people could form a procession, and do that in two directions, as coming and going, as indicated by the tiny arrows in a following illustration (fig. 4).

---

4. Claudel. *Le Soulier de Satin*. (prologue to Act 1)

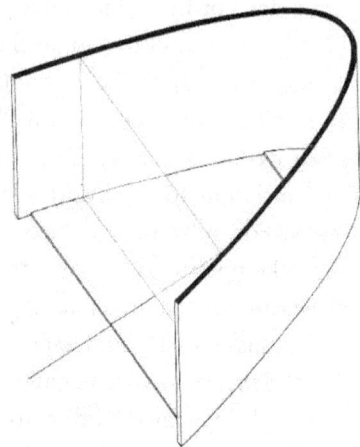

FIGURE 2. *The Church Incarnate*, page 159. The parabola as wall.

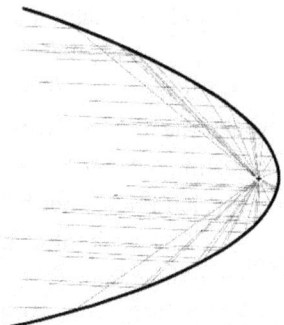

FIGURE 3. *The Church Incarnate*, page 174. The parabola as reflector.

FIGURE 4. *The Church Incarnate*, page 175. The parabola as pathway.

The Foundation

Clearly these must be conceptions of different realities. As an engineer my attention had been focused on the single reality of an objective, ordered, and predictable non-quantum universe, but in studying Schwarz's book I experienced how multiple worlds may co-exist. This expansion has important implications for architecture, design and theology, but he does not make it easy. I followed him as best I could, being dragged through swamps, led up blind alleys and having to leap over chasms, but I had the sense that the journey was a Sacred Journey, with a worthwhile goal of service, not at the end but along the way. To assist other seekers I offer this work, not as a substitute for Schwarz's work but as a companion to it. Guardini himself felt that a companion volume would be useful, saying[5]: "This is a book about which one could write a much larger book . . . it seems to me that it should be possible to translate the deep thoughts of this writing into a very simple language."

Instead of the "much larger book" Guardini mentioned, it's my ambition to attempt a book which, by the clarity of its "very simple language," could be much smaller. Compared to *The Church Incarnate* this work that I am offering is both more and less. More: because it bridges gaps and makes connections that Schwarz only hinted at, and less: because it avoids attractive detours and seductive dead-ends where he sometimes gets bogged-down. And all the while, on the way, a companion offers friendship and the agreement that there is a common goal. In this case, the goal is for the knowledge and insights picked up along the way to be useful; to be of service to humanity.

In his very first sentence Schwarz writes that the spirit may find its expression in multiple physical forms, and a physical form may have multiple spiritual significances. He notes that in former times the term "the body of Christ" could be applied to many things: to an altar, to the congregation, to the building where the people meet, or to the whole earth. And for him, as for those ancient congregations, these were not metaphors, they were descriptions of a reality that was layered with holiness. Thus the worship space in a church building, looked-upon as Christ's body, was perceived as a real body. The space in the chancel was the head, the transepts were the outstretched arms, the body was the nave, and the crossing was the

---

5. Guardini, see Foreword

heart. Tradition states that when Jesus died on the cross his head fell to the left, so in some medieval churches the chancel was also turned slightly to the left, creating a so-called "weeping chancel."

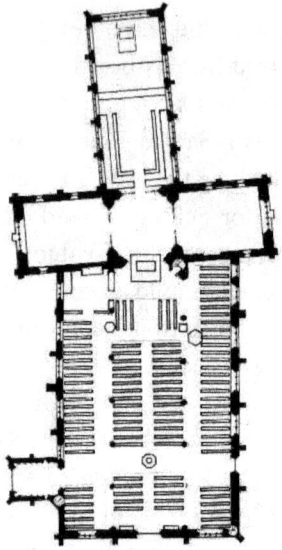

FIGURE 5. The Church of the Holy Trinity, Stratford-upon-Avon. A natural response for us when we are in such a church is for us too to turn our heads slightly to the left; a gentle offering of ourselves to share an experience and express a unity with the Savior.

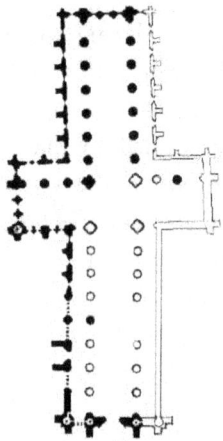

FIGURE 6. The ruins of Whitby Abbey also reveal a Weeping Chancel.

If present-day congregations are made aware of this ancient wisdom they too can share in these experiences. The Church of the Holy Trinity in Stratford-upon-Avon is an example of this. The plan clearly shows how the chancel is inclined. In Europe over forty examples of this layout have been recorded—in all of them the chancel is tilted to the left, none to the right.

Recently I stumbled across another example when watching a re-run of an episode of a British ITV drama "Heartbeat" which takes place in Yorkshire. In that episode a meeting was to take place among the ruins of Whitby Abbey, and a brief aerial overview of the 13th Century ruins revealed that here too, as in fig. 6, the choir was tilted to the left.

There are some vestiges of this ancient wisdom that survive into our present day—notably that we regard it as quite normal to build churches with transepts (even if they are not functional) protruding from the sides of the church.

FIGURE 7. The doors to the Church of Santa Sabina in Rome.

In 432 CE the cypress-wood doors of the Church of Santa Sabina in Rome were decorated with carved panels depicting various biblical scenes, among them one of the Crucifixion. Here the cross does not have a prominent presence, indicating that the cross itself had not achieved importance as a symbol, and it would not be used as a generator for the plans of cruciform churches for another several centuries.

In the interval the form of the cross changed, and became the familiar symbol we have today: a vertical post with a horizontal crossbar attached slightly above center. It is most unlikely that a cross of this form would ever have been used for crucifixions. Anyone with experience in carpentry will know that this is a very unsatisfactory way to make a joint to sustain a vertical load. If the two timbers are nailed together the entire weight is borne by the nails and the connection is wobbly. If one member is notched into the other this requires careful workmanship and both members are weakened at the point of maximum stress. Much more practical is the T-shaped cross (or Tau cross, named for the Greek letter Tau) where the crosspiece sits on a spike embedded in the top of the shaft. If the spike protrudes it could also be used for affixing a notice. There is support for this in the apocryphal Epistle of Barnabas[6], a contender in the early church for inclusion in the New Testament. It bases its argument on gematria, the process for creating a numeric value for a phrase from scripture. This is possible because there were no numerals in Hebrew or Greek, the languages of the old and new testaments, so letters were substituted, as in the following table. In this system Tau represents the number 300.

$$1 = α, \ 2 = β, \ 3 = γ, \ 4 = δ, \ 5 = ε, \ 7 = ζ, \ 8 = η, \ 9 = θ,$$

$$10 = ι, \ 20 = κ, \ 30 = λ, \ 40 = μ, \ 50 = ν, \ 60 = ξ, \ 70 = ο, \ 80 = π,$$

$$100 = ρ, \ 200 = σ, \ 300 = τ, \ 400 = υ, \ 500 = φ, \ 600 = χ, \ 700 = ψ, \ 800 = ω.$$

Thus a word or phrase could be given a numeric significance by adding the numeric values of its letters. Here's Barnabas: chapter 8, verses 10–13 in the William Hone translation, re-numbered as chapter 9, verses 6 and 7 in the J.B. Lightfoot translation:

> 10. Understand, therefore, children, these things more fully, that Abraham, who was the first that brought in circumcision, looking forward in the Spirit to Jesus, circumcised, having received the mystery of three letters.

---

6. Hone, Apocrypha, 152.

11. For the scripture says that Abraham circumcised three hundred and eighteen men of his house. But what therefore was the mystery that was made known unto him?

12. Note first the eighteen and next the three hundred. For the numeral letters of ten and eight are I H, and these denote Jesus.

13. And because the cross was that by which we were to find grace; therefore he adds three hundred; the note of which is T (the figure of his cross.) Wherefore by two letters he signified Jesus, and by the third his cross.

FIGURE 8. Hans Multscher depicts the cross as a "T."

Even if this exercise in gematria, which attempts to find in Genesis a foreshadowing of Jesus, should appear to be a little far-fetched there can be no doubt that the author of this ancient text, written between 70 and 130 CE, knew that the common form of the cross of crucifixion was in the form of a T because he relates the cross to the number 300 and it is Tau that has this numerical value.

However with the passing of the Roman Empire people no longer had first-hand knowledge of crucifixions, and what was considered to be the form of its instrument of executions morphed into the shape with which we are familiar, although there have been some exceptions, such as in the work of Hans Multscher, Giotto, and Fra Angelico, who still acknowledged the physicalness of the Tau-cross.

FIGURE 9. A Trophy of Triumph.

From such a cross the body would hang down from the wrists in the form of a Y. A person standing in this bodily posture, with the arms raised above the head, would be seen as expressing triumph.

That could be the posture of a politician acknowledging his election. It is the way a commander fires-up his troops. It depicts a preacher dominating his congregation. But Christ's crucifixion was not a triumph over his enemies, it was a humble acceptance of his fate, where he forgave his opponents in an act of reconciliation and love. To portray this forgiving aspect his head would be erect and his arms outstretched in a gesture of welcome. This is the way we imagine the father of the Prodigal Son, his arms spread wide in welcome and forgiveness and joy at the return of his son. So to represent the crucifixion as an act of atonement the form of the cross had to be modified from the Tau cross into a form which matches the posture of Christ's forgiving body, the form with which we are familiar today. In fact the cross had become a symbol or token for the Body of Christ, his outstretched arms forgiving us and inviting us to be his church.

The Foundation

So when we build a church with transepts, and that is quite commonplace, we are not just building a church in the form of a cross—that would just be creating a symbol of a symbol—we are making manifest the Body of Christ. Rudolf Schwarz mentions this in *The Church Incarnate*, on page 3 in the 9th line. (We have to specify the line because on occasion Schwarz makes contrasting statements on the same page, so references will be indicated in the format of "(3, line 9)." These are cross-referenced in a table at the back of the book, so if you are reading Schwarz and come across a passage that is difficult you could perhaps find it elucidated in this companion. You might also find it useful to make a line-counter by photocopying a typical page from Schwarz's book, numbering all the lines, and cutting the page into a strip to use as a bookmark—this could save a lot of counting of lines.

In medieval times the cross on the altar or communion table would be a token of the Body of Christ; the five crosses carved into its top surface indicating his five wounds. The processional cross would indicate that we are following Christ, and the stone cross that tops-off the steeple would indicate we are all under his authority. Schwarz embraced this medieval consciousness of the immediacy of Christ in all things. It is the unfamiliarity of this mindset that makes his works so difficult for us to read and yet so valuable. We are continuously challenged.

Perhaps, rather than as a "church architect" we should regard Schwarz as "a designing theologian." To learn from him we have to meet him where he is. We have to accept, as far as we are able, his sense of the immediacy of the spirit. He did not set out to express the spirit in his buildings, his buildings were an embodiment of the spirit in physical matter, they were spirit-made-solid; and because the spirit lives and is ever and always new, in each age our worship spaces must spring forth in a new experience of birth. We cannot recapture a medieval piety by recreating a medieval building. In particular we have to be careful with the cross. In some senses it has now become a symbol of division. We have difficulty seeing it in the medieval manner as the underlying form of the Body of Christ. It has taken on the role of a heraldic symbol that distinguishes our religion from other religions. The Knights Templar, those warrior-monks, had crosses embroidered on their tunics when they set out to slaughter the infidels, and cenotaphs or war memorials were often topped-off with a cross to celebrate that in the bloody conflict God was on our side. This triumph is still proclaimed in such hymns as "Lift High the Cross," which envisages a world conquest where we are the conquerors. The cross can have many roles; bear many messages. From his own experiences as an architect Rudolf Schwarz comments at length on this (205, line 9 to 206) and in this he expresses himself with admirable clarity, offering a rare glimpse into his personality.

So indeed we must be cautious in our use of the cross as it is capable of transmitting mixed messages. As a geometrical figure it could have many interpretations, and many of these could be unintended or inappropriate. The figure itself is ambiguous: does it represent two lines crossing as in a crucifix, or four lines radiating from a point as in the axes of a cruciform church? Should its plane be vertical as an object of veneration, or should it be horizontal as setting out directions or pathways, or does it matter? This calls for caution.

The illustration of the doors of the Church of Santa Sabina shows the crucified Christ being almost twice the size of the two thieves alongside him. As Schwarz notes (5, line 28) the relative size of the figures reflects their relative importance in a convention that was available to medieval artists. When in the 14th Century the rules of perspective were codified[7] a new convention emerged, and the relative size of subjects became an indication of their closeness to the observer. Perspective fixed one's presence to a single viewpoint, so it was no longer possible to enter the work. The observer of the painting or sculpture then sees a human view of what a creator of the work observed, he being a particular person standing at a particular point in space and time.

With its focus on a human response to what is seen by a particular human, a work of art is almost a self-portrait, perhaps beautifully rendered but restricted in what it can portray. In contrast, the medieval artist is not limited to a particular point in space and time, so he is free to express a closeness to God. He can express a multitude of meanings in the world of the spirit. In this world Schwarz found it comfortable to live and move and have his being. That is what makes his writing both so difficult and so valuable.

Some of this ancient consciousness persists today in the icons which make an important contribution to the worship of the Orthodox

---

7. Giotto di Bondone (1277-1337)

Communions. Here the style of painting is a given and it is the size and placement of the images that is meaningful. Thus the infant Christ is sometimes presented as a miniature version of a fully developed man to communicate a promise of his future glory while still a little child. Iconographers are seen, not as painters, but as icon writers (that is the root meaning of the word) so icons are narratives. They are interpreted as literature in the medium of pigment, egg, and gold leaf.

In the world of the spirit, which Schwarz is comfortable to inhabit, "inside" and "outside" are interchangeable because the presence that infuses that world is universal. Schwarz could see how humans could approach, within the church, the throne of heavenly grace, but he could also see how God could embrace the church as a vessel for his dear people, and that in a world of his creation. This was an ancient awareness which we in our secular world have lost. God so loved the world—but we don't! As a species we pollute it with our consumption, our waste, and our presence, while keeping God safely sequestered in a structure with charitable status, tax exemption, and an historic designation where we gather for about one hour per week. The spirit has been banished to a small corner of our lives. It is no wonder that the church has become for many of us irrelevant, or what is worse, antique. For the church to cease to be irrelevant we need to change our minds, but for it to cease to be antique we need to change what the church has become.

The Body and the Building

In his first five pages Schwarz has been pondering on what is meant by describing the Church as the Body of Christ. He notes that in medieval times we had a different perception of ourselves and the world we live in. We perceived the world, and everything in it, ourselves included, as being threaded-through with the spirit. Thus the body was process rather than object, a participant in the flux of the universe. It was "a work to be continually accomplished between God and the Soul." (7, line 29) Thus the Body of Christ was a real body, as real as ours. That was possible because what constituted reality in those days differed from our current perceptions. Even the words they used in those days to describe the world had different meanings from what we understand by them today. For us the old words no longer name the same living reality (9, line 26). However, that reality still exists, it is still real, and Schwarz believes "that the sacred objectivity of those old concepts is true, and we will ourselves have to be converted to it." (8, line 11) He advocates not that we return to an historical mindset but that in all things we recognize the holiness of God's creation, including finding it in ourselves. For the remainder of his first chapter, The Foundation, Schwarz proposes how this could be achieved for our present age, how we could acquire a God-centered sensibility and with this bring into being a God-centered church. He approaches both the body and building from a standpoint that acknowledges the spirituality of each, but in contemporary terms. With this approach he investigates the spiritual significance of the body by musing on the receptive function of the eye and the light that it admits, and the creative function of the hand; devoting a section to each. Perhaps he was influenced in this by a quotation[8] from Goethe: "The hands want to see, the eyes want to caress."

Schwarz catalogs the works of the hand in creating works of art and works of construction. His analysis commences with an acknowledgment of the beauty of the eye (11, line 27) but before we plunge into his text I would like to point out an example of the incredible power of this work. His book is the core text for "Shaping Space for Worship," a course which I teach at Trinity College in Toronto. In this course several students have chosen to seek ordination, having reported that his insights changed their lives. Evidence for this power can be found in the "Translator's Invitation" which forms a preface to *The Church Incarnate*. Here the translator, Cynthia Harris, shows how she has internalized Schwarz's teachings when she invokes for herself his spiritual concepts[9] for the roles of the Eye, the Light, and the Hand, where she addresses the reader, saying: "You are probably sitting in a chair with the sun streaming over your shoulder, let us hope, or at least with a lamp at your side. With your hand you hold this book and your eye is running over the page . . ." If you will allow this to describe your present situation we will now explore Schwarz's concepts for body, light, eye and hand.

---

8. Goethe, J. W. von. *"Die Hände wollen sehen, die Augen streicheln"*

9. Harris, *Translator's Invitation*.

The Foundation

The Eye

This section begins with an essay on the propagation of light in which Schwarz identifies three elements:
>The generating center—what he calls "star,"
>The rays of light, and what he calls
>The sphere of light, the extent of that radiation.

This he illustrates this with a diagram on page 12.

These elements would be familiar to a medieval audience. Source, shining and sphere are found in a poem[10] by John Donne where he upbraids the sun that bids him rise and vacate the blissful embrace of the languorous Mrs. Donne.

>"Busie old foole, unruly sunne,
>
>Why dost thou thus,
>
>Through windowes and through curtaines call on us?
>
>… Shine here to us, and thou art everywhere:
>
>This bed thy centre is, these walls thy spheare."

Schwarz's approach is certainly poetic, and he takes up a lot of space expounding it, but that does not match the holy awe that we feel when science reveals the wonder of light being simultaneously wave and particle in a quantum universe; a body of knowledge that was just being made available in Schwarz's lifetime. Science does not say what light "is": it just reports that in examining it we receive these responses that may have contradictory interpretations. In fact Schwarz shows some agreement with this assertion (3, line 16) when he states that "the little word 'is' remains completely open and ready to exist at the most varied levels." Although he does not mention it in his text there is an irony that the diagram Schwarz created could be taken as illustrating this duality, showing both a radiating stream of particles and a coherent circular wave-front.

Perhaps we have some innate sense of this duality when in the ordinary language of conversation we might remark that light can bathe an object (as if it were a wave) or light can strike an object (as if it were a rain of particles).

---

10. Donne, *The Sunne Rising*, 1633.

Being aware of this duality we experience light as a spiritual concept far more engaging than a mere geometrical construct. Science, in its appreciation of the cosmos, may be more spiritual than theology.

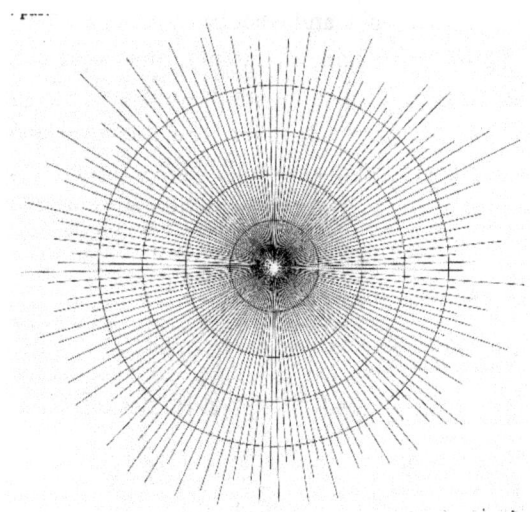

FIGURE 10. *The Church Incarnate*, page 12. Light shines.

The diagram that follows is a bit difficult to understand. It suffers from the limitation that for his book Schwarz used black ink to depict white light, so the immediate impression of his illustration (fig. 11) is that of a magician's wand.

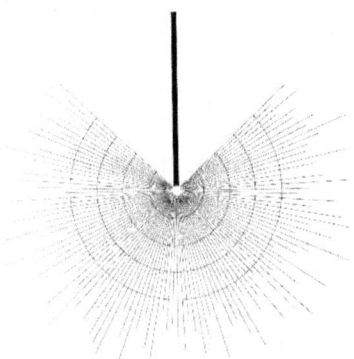

FIGURE 11. Light spreads from an illuminated object. *The Church Incarnate*, page 13.

The Foundation

Inverting the image black-to-white helps a bit to clarify its purpose, which is to show how the light from a source can illuminate an object which then becomes a secondary source of light that can enter the eye. The "wand" becomes a source of light only as long as it is bathed in light from the primary source. The intent of the diagram is to illustrate the trajectory of light "from source to object to eye." This enables the eye to both see the object and assume the existence of the original source. The eye does not see the source, but the illuminated object affirms its presence. In this way a well-wrought church can affirm for us the presence of God in the world.

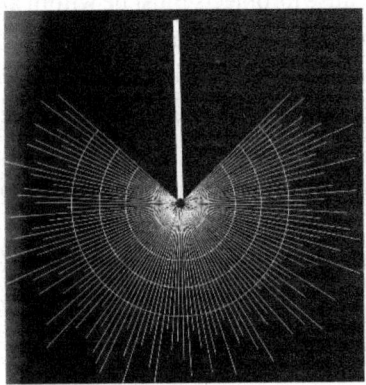

FIGURE 12. The image inverted.

The trajectory is God-to-Christ-to-World where the Body of Christ is the church; or, putting it another way

> The Father sends the Son into the World, where
>
> The Son sends forth Man to be his Church in the Father's World.

Schwarz notes that the eye receives the light which, projected on the retina, creates an image. This image is not of the whole illuminated object (15, line 10). The eye can only see the image of that face which an object presents to it—reality exists beyond what is visible to the eye. The retina is an evaginated surface of the brain, so it is possible for the image to be interpreted. The image may have meaning, and that meaning may extend beyond what we see. Thus the object that generates an image may have significance as a symbol. If, for us, that significance is holy, what we happen to see is a sacrament: an outward and visible sign of an inner and spiritual grace.

The Hand

By its sense of touch the hand can also see (19, line 15). It is able to see both more and less than the eye—more because it can also observe the backs of things, and less because its objects must be within arms' length. In human relationships the hand is expressive, more expressive than the eye. The open palm may caress another, the closed fist may strike a blow. We are aware of a multitude of hand signals that might indicate acceptance or rejection, support or disdain.

The hand can also manipulate physical reality, but for this it must be directed by the eye. The partnership of hand and eye is creative. Schwarz lists its potential in creating works of art (24, line 12). He also notes that in erecting a building "a whole ordered company of men takes part" (27, line 3) and indeed, in English, workers may be referred to as "hands."

Perceiving Space

The hand has another ability not given to the eye—it can "perceive" space. The eye cannot do this. Light passes through space unimpeded so space cannot be seen. All that the eye can do is to see objects on the other side of a space, and where there is the most space there is, in that emptiness, the least to see. The hand however can sense gaps between objects. With the assistance of a reaching arm it can extend its range, and as part of a mobile body it can reach even farther. The reaching body is the way we perceive space. How then do we define space?

In the *Toronto Journal of Theology*[11] I suggested that we can derive some clues for how we perceive space from the ways we describe it. Take for

---

11. Robinson, "Liturgical Architecture."

example a very high space such as the main hall at Grand Central Terminal in Manhattan. We would describe this space as soaring, uplifting, releasing.

If we consider a very low space, such as the Basilica Pius X, the underground shrine at Lourdes in France, we would describe this space as crushing, oppressing (and please note that these photographs are depicting the context for the space, not the space itself).

Finally, if we take a very long space, such as the long passageway at the South Kensington Station on the London Underground, we could describe that space as stretching, extending. What all these descriptions have in common is that they are all verbs, they all relate to things we can do with our bodies. We can leap and soar and crush and stretch. These are all human capabilities. Of course we are not really stretched and crushed. No matter how I stretched I could not reach the twenty foot high ceiling at Lourdes while feeling that sensation of a crushing weight overhead, and in Grand Central Station I walk on the floor like everybody else while feeling like flying. Space is described in terms of our bodies. We imagine what we would have to do in order to experience what we perceive as the quality of the space, and then we describe the space as if it were itself performing these actions. It is truly wonderful that space, the most immaterial quantity we can imagine, is experienced by our bodies, our closest contact with the material world. Space is best expressed as a verb: it can dance and sing, space can laugh, space can wonder, space can worship. Schwarz agrees, saying (212, line 15):

> "Church building is 'work which prays,' work which is borne by the movement of grace."

Space speaks to us. And if it can speak to us space must have a language, and that language is evidence of meaning. The joy of architecture, going beyond mere building, is the human emotions it generates as responses to its expressions of space. This possibility was noted by Rudolf Schwarz in a single short sentence—just four words: "Space is dancingly experienced," (27, line 12) but instead of pursuing this concept he wanders off into another discussion. I find this Journey with him inspiring but also frustrating. Time-and-again he almost gets to a conclusion, and then he drops it and moves off in another direction. Perhaps it's the purpose of this work to connect the dots, to provide the connective tissue that will put him back on track when he wanders off course. A journey is not a walk: a journey has a route and a destination, while the purpose for a walk is the experiences it offers in passing.

Schwarz did not have a clear view of his destination—about his book he writes (31, line 9) "All these things are thoughts which occurred to us about our own work," and such thoughts might be random. He breaks up his journey with frequent side trips which may reveal great beauty but leave the reader confused. It is the job of the Companion to await his return from these wanderings, and with a map to gently set him back on a course where the world can benefit greatly from his wisdom, as have I. He does not make it easy. These detours make it hard for the reader to determine "what the book's about"; which perhaps explains why, in spite of having had so much respect in the world, he has had so little real influence. Schwarz uses the language of space to communicate a spiritual meaning: a language embedded in the spaces formed by his tiny models, those which he calls his Plans.

His first chapter ends with a discussion of various construction methods (27, line 21): shell, sculpture, skeleton, tent. This is not strictly necessary for his thesis but we must remember that he wrote these words in the 1920s. At that time there was a revolution and "modern architecture" was just coming into being, with a new focus on integrity after a hundred years of 19th century pastiche. He remarks (22, line 32) "Work can be true work only if it grows out of what is real". Structure which had previously been obscured by a superficial layering of decoration could now be revealed as true in its own right.

This struggle was an important part of Rudolf Schwarz's evolution as an architect, and because it was so important to him he spends seven pages describing the significance of various structural options. Beyond saying "Building . . . is first and foremost circumscribed space," (27, line 5) he does not go so far as to mention the importance of space, although in his work he was certainly conscious of it. We can forgive this neglected opportunity because we have inherited his beautiful buildings where clear light washing across plain surfaces reveals functional clarity and structural integrity. In his work he shows a wish for building to be well-done: in particular for church buildings to be an offering of love and service to the Creator, matching as far as humanly possible the perfection of God's creation. For a church the physical building is a sacrifice, its space a sacrament.

The Foundation

Figure 13. A high space in Grand Central Station.

Figure 14. The lowering of the subterranean Basilica Pius X at Lourdes.

Figure 15. A long space in the London Underground.

Schwarz would have loved the logic that space is experienced by the body because from this it follows that the space in Christ's church is an expression of the Body of Christ.

PART II
The First Six Plans

In Part II of his book Schwarz offers diagrams of various liturgical arrangements and observes how they will impact the worship of congregations. He offers over forty variations, but to be manageable he gathers them up into six categories of structures which correspond to varying degrees of open-ness ranging from a solid dome to a totally open structure—a series of models which he calls The First Six Plans.

There is much misunderstanding over the role of The First Six Plans *(Die sechs ersten Plane)*. The words "sechs Plane" could mean either "Six ways of going forward, as in six intentions," or "Six indications of the physical form of a building." With this confusion many have assumed that his drawings of the Six Plans are ideal forms for church buildings, with the development sequence of spirit-to-Plan-to-building. In this they are quite mistaken. Schwarz himself was deeply opposed to this interpretation of his work, saying (227, line 23) "The Plans are . . . not to be copied but to grow up once more as new." His purpose was to enable church buildings to support Christian worship, but because he was a devout Catholic he felt that in designing churches his own architectural work had to comply with the religious doctrines of the day, so he did not allow himself to build any of his Six Plans. He became quite angry when his Fifth Plan (see fig. 2, or Schwarz page 159) was used for the construction of the Heilig-Kreuz church in Bottrop.

I find it most useful to regard the First Six Plans as icons—as physical expressions of spiritual truths. In this they fulfill the role of icons in the Orthodox Church, which are seen not as works of art but as statements of spiritual truths presented in physical form. Similarly, it is these truths themselves, rather than the way they are represented, that should guide the construction of worship space. When I visualize them I see his Plans as two-dimensional drawings for the imagining of small 3D models, each about the size of a teapot, and perhaps made of ceramic. Schwarz gives support to this concept when he describes two of his Plans as "chalices" (95, line 3; and 154, line 3). These models, by virtue of the spaces they contain, are able to embody and express spiritual truths; they are the medium which Schwarz, as an architect, uses to communicate spiritual values. It is these truths, and not the form of the Plans, that can generate architectural plans that will incorporate such truths into the design of a physical building. Such a building will generate spaces that enshrine and enable those original spiritual values—they will transform a building into a church (vom Bau der Kirche). The sequence would be:

> from the Spirit
>
> to a Plan (one of the Six)
>
> to the Spirit (as revealed in that Plan)
>
> to a plan (made by an architect)
>
> to a building (with solid walls)
>
> to a space (created by those walls)
>
> to an experience of the Spirit.

To go directly from Plan to building negates this process. If the Plans were mere building plans they would not be capable of carrying the spirit—the building thus created would just be a very large version of a model. The Plans are a language that Schwarz uses for communication, and it is the insights he is able to express by this language that are of value, not the form of the language itself.

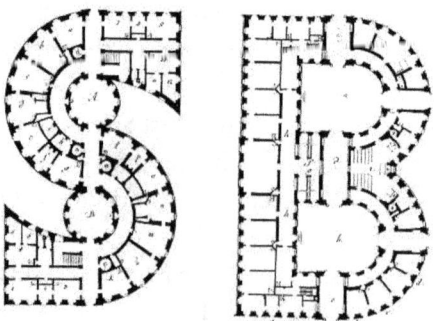

FIGURE 16. Alphabet Houses. Plans published by Johann David Steingruber.

Examples of the downside of giving buildings a form that is symbolic of a means of communication can be seen in the letter-form houses designed by Johann Steingruber. He was a building inspector for the Prince of

The First Six Plans

Brandenburg-Anspach in Bavaria, and in 1773 he published a whole alphabet of them. He felt a palace could honor its prince by being built in the form of his initials, and likewise a church could acknowledge its patron saint. But we have to ask ourselves what sorts of buildings would result and

FIGURE 17. Workers' housing in Caracas, Venezuela, in the form of the initials of its architect. The "C" is represented by the most distant building in the photograph, the "V" is closest. The drawing is by Victor Mantilla-Bazo.

what sort of feelings would they elicit? Once we get past the elegant façades we see a conglomeration of miserable, odd-shaped rooms, tortuous corridors, and claustrophobic courtyards. At best they are whimsical, and at worst oppressive; not the qualities we would wish to see in a place of worship.

In Venezuela there is a grouping of buildings in the form of letters that actually did get built. This is the 1948 workers housing development, El Silencio, in downtown Caracas, which overlooks the principal square in Caracas, also called El Silencio. These four-story concrete buildings are built in the form of the letters C, R, and V, (see figure 17) which are the initials of Carlos Raul Villanueva, the architect for the development. Villanueva was one of the most loved and respected architects in South America and it is possible that the spaces created by his buildings did not suffer by being constrained to spell out the initials of his name. However, even if the design were motivated by a wish to serve, even if it were not an exercise in self-aggrandizement, it still represents a formalistic oppression which could only be visited on the poor or the powerless.

Why Six?

In Part II of his book, "The First Six Plans," Schwarz illustrates over forty plans, which he groups into six categories. First we should ask ourselves: "Why six?"

Of course, forty varieties would be impractical to deal with; in fact if there were more than a dozen groupings their categories would be so divers the list would probably constitute a catalog rather than an identification of communities. So going to six, half-way to twelve, would be a reasonable and practical outcome. However Schwarz was not always constrained by being reasonable and practical, and for a reason that would be more likely to motivate him we have to look elsewhere. Plans are a record of a possibility or an intention to create, and what comes to mind in his decision to select six as the number of his plans is that in Genesis God allotted six days for the creation of the universe. In the fifth century St. Augustine of Hippo[12] in his monumental *City of God* wrote:

---

12. St. Augustine, *City of God*. 30.

The First Six Plans

"The works of Creation are described as being repeated six times. The reason for this is that six is the number of perfection . . . it is the first number, as I have said, which is made up of the sum of its factors, and in this number God brought his works to complete perfection. Hence the theory of number is not to be lightly regarded since it is made quite clear in many passages of the Holy Scriptures how highly it is to be regarded . . . God, who could have created the world in an instant, instead chose to do it in six days, because six is the number of perfection."

Perfect numbers are those which are equal to the sum of their factors (a factor is a number that evenly divides a larger number). Thus six is a perfect number because its factors, 1, 2, and 3, add up to 6. The next perfect number is 28, as its factors are 1, 2, 4, 7 and 14, and the sum of these is 28. This is followed by 496, 8128, 33,550,336 . . . in a rapidly expanding infinite series, all of whose values end in a 6 or an 8.

The poetic association of the number six with creation could have influenced Schwarz to make that his choice for organizing his work; but many years after his book was published I discovered a more compelling reason[13] for the choice of "Six," but one that needs a bit of unpacking: it is that worship too expresses itself in exactly six ministries, and these ministries could be the organizing focus of six clusters of plans.

For Schwarz a Plan is the spiritual expression of a response to the needs of a congregation, so if we can show that congregational worship presents itself in six distinct ministries, that would be a rationale he could have used for his choice of six Plans. Basing the Six Plans on the six ministries of worship would create a much more rigorous framework because, paradoxically, buildings which we feel to be solid and unmovable are in fact soft and malleable but ministries are not. You can always adjust a building; by making it a little bit longer or a little bit shorter, block up windows or open-up doors, add to the sides or demolish from the center, until the building takes on a totally different character, moving from one category to another—but ministries are defined by words, and are therefore immutable. What follows is an exposition that all worship is expressed in exactly six ministries, and these correspond to Schwarz's Six Plans.

13. Robinson, *Rebuilding the Church on a New Foundation*, 34.

The Six Ministries of Worship

Worship is the expression and celebration of a revered relationship of praise and thanksgiving; a relationship between

> the People,
>
> the Sacraments, and
>
> the World.

These are the three parameters[14], or defining terms or entities, in Christian worship. I'll call them parameters. To define these parameters.

The **People** are those gathered to hear and proclaim the Word, and to share in Holy Communion.

What is a **Sacrament**? Those of us who had to learn their catechism from the old Book of Common Prayer will remember a sacrament as being "an outward and visible sign of an inner and spiritual grace." The Sacraments of Baptism and Holy Communion and the readings of scripture are channels by which God's grace is imparted to us.

The **World** is the totality of God's creation, the context of our humanity.

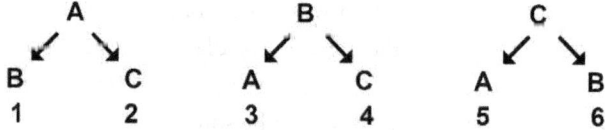

FIGURE 18. A tree of relationships.

Worship is about relationship. This term, relationship, also occurs in mathematics. If we apply the mathematics of permutations to the three parameters of worship we find that there are six, and only six, possible relationships between them. That is: these three parameters, taken two-at-a-time, may be combined into exactly six permutations, each of which

---

14. A parameter is a factor whose value determines the form or character of an operation.

expresses a unique relationship. From this we can deduce that there are six ways in which worship can express itself.

The mathematical underpinning for the six expressions of worship can be demonstrated (see fig. 18) by creating a tree, rather like a family tree, showing there are six possible relationships between pairs of three parameters, here indicated by the letters A, B, and C.

Relationship is a vector, which means it has a direction. Thus the relationship of A-to-B is not the same as the relationship of B-to-A. As an example, my relationship to you, dear Reader, is not the same as your relationship to me. My relationship to you consists of my making a unique Body of Knowledge available to you for your information, instruction, and delight. Crudely put, your relationship to me involves your paying a considerable amount of cash to my publishers in the hope that some of it may trickle down to me.

This mathematical computation is valuable because by establishing that the three parameters of worship may be combined in six, and only six, relationships we know we have defined the field. We have established that Christian worship may occur in six, and only six, distinct ministries, and these embrace all the possibilities for worship. Knowing this, we don't have to cast about looking for a seventh ministry. Anything that looks like a seventh ministry will turn out to be a thinly-disguised version of one of the other six.

What are these ministries? By considering the qualities of each relationship between parameters we can deduce which ministry it represents. The six ministries are set out in order of the presence and focus of the worshipers, ranging from the introspective ministry of Contemplation to the extremely extroverted ministry of Justice.

The Six Ministries

Here are set out the six ministries formed by the pairing of parameters:

1. For the first ministry the relationship is: **People-to-Sacrament**.

    The People approach the Sacrament with awe, to adore and meditate on the divine presence. This is the ministry of **Contemplation.**

2. For the second the relationship is: **Sacrament-to-People**.

    The Sacrament is brought to the People to heal, forgive, reconcile and bless. This is the ministry of **Pastoral Care**.

3. For the third ministry the relationship is: **Sacrament-to-World**.

    The light of the Sacrament shines out into the World, to proclaim Christ's presence. This is the ministry of **Witness**.

4. For the fourth ministry the relationship is: **World-to-People**.

    The World becomes a path for the People, who band themselves together for a common purpose. This is the ministry of **Dedication**.

5. For the fifth ministry the relationship is: **World-to-Sacrament**.

    The World is invited to approach and share the Sacrament and share in communion with Christ. This is the ministry of **Evangelism**.

6. For the sixth ministry the relationship is: **People-to-World**.

    The People go out into the World to secure justice, peace, freedom, and fulfillment for all. This is the ministry of **Justice**.

These six relationships yield the ministries of Contemplation, Pastoral Care, Witness, Dedication, Evangelism, and Justice.

The Formation of the Plans

Because we now know the relationships that constitute each of the Six Ministries we are able to sift through Schwarz's collection of individual plans and assemble for each Plan the version which best serves each ministry—sometimes this might require a new Plan created from a fusion of features taken from various other examples. Each Plan is not a model for construction, as Schwarz has warned (227, line 24):

> "The Plans are a genuine happening which has withdrawn utterly into its own potentiality, which has become wholly seed and beginning and waits, not to be copied down again, but to grow up once more as new."

The First Six Plans

It is truly a wonderment that each of Schwarz's Six Plans, formulated in a mystical vision, corresponds in number, order, and content, to a member of the array of the Six Ministries of the Christian church which I deduced from a mathematical analysis. There is an implication here that these could be individual expressions of a universal principle that invests all creation.

Before we consider each individual Plan I should point out there is a problem with the naming of them. Schwarz gives each Plan a name that could describe some aspect of the form of its physical structure rather than its liturgical function. Some of his titles are idiosyncratic if not contradictory, and some of the English translations of these are ambiguous—for example "parting" can refer to a rent or an event, and "cast" has different meanings for the sculptor and the angler, and it is not immediately apparent which of these meanings is intended—and he gives the name "Parting" to two of his Plans, the second and the third, whose liturgical functions are quite different. I would love to be creative and acknowledge each of Schwarz's Plans by giving each an appropriate name but I fear this would just add to the existing confusion. Only the names he has given to the first and fourth plans accurately reflect their functions, so to avoid duplication I will abandon the poetic luxury of renaming his plans and restrict myself to referring to all the plans just by their numbers and their associated ministries.

These problems arose because at the time Schwarz did not have a logical system for classifying his Plans. In a sense, it could be possible to dispense with considering any Plans at all, and just list the spatial requirements for six ministries. This might satisfy some theoreticians, but church builders like myself are practical people, and we would appreciate being given an archetypal plan which we could study as a jumping-off-point for creativity. We now begin a study of Schwarz's Six Plans.

The First Plan for the Ministry of Contemplation

I would have loved to have used Schwarz's title "Sacred Inwardness" for this consideration of the first of his Six Plans—it's such a beautifully descriptive title. However I would then have to use titles for the other five plans, and most of those titles would differ from, or even contradict, the titles Rudolf Schwarz selected for them, so in the interests of clarity, and with profound regret, I will just refer to the plans by number and ministry, as in the heading above.

Schwarz founded his model for The First Plan on simple beginnings: on a family sitting around the dinner table, on a meeting of the Early Church in somebody's home, or on the Last Supper. He writes (36, line 1) "We must enter into the simple things at the source of the Christian life. We must begin anew, and our new beginning must be genuine." These "simple things" are space, community, table, bread, cup, and light—the illustration is taken from my *Rebuilding the Church on a New Foundation,* and lists the six elements (clockwise from 1 o'clock).

FIGURE 19. Elements of the First Eucharist.

THE FIRST PLAN

Each of these elements has become a powerful symbol, enriching our experience of the Eucharist.

The first Christian church building that we know of, that is, the first building built specifically as a church, is the Mary Chapel at Glastonbury[15], built in 64 AD. This was a dome-like structure "of wandes and branches" built by twelve monks sent to Avalon from Gaul by St. Philip. The monks made a ring of holes, a ring 39.6 feet in diameter, in which they set saplings. These they bent over and laced together with vines to create a structure like an igloo or an Indian sweat-lodge.

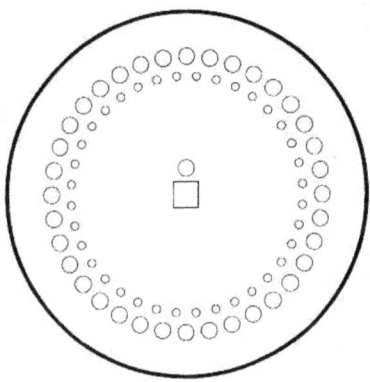

FIGURE 20. The First Plan, for the Ministry of Contemplation.

This was the first purpose-built Christian church. In it the people could gather in a ring around a central table to contemplate the divine presence in the celebration of the Eucharist. The illustration shows the essentials: the space, the people, and the table; and on the table are the bread, the wine, and the candles. It's such a joy to be able to go all the way back to the first Christian church to establish the model for our First Plan.

Schwarz's illustration for this Plan on page 37 of his book shows a much more grandiose structure. The dome is huge—over one hundred feet in diameter. The altar is raised on three steps, a convention of a doctrine that did not appear until the fifth century; and it is surrounded by 361 worshipers—I've counted them. The early Christians would be amazed.

---

15. Michell, *City of Revelation*, 45.

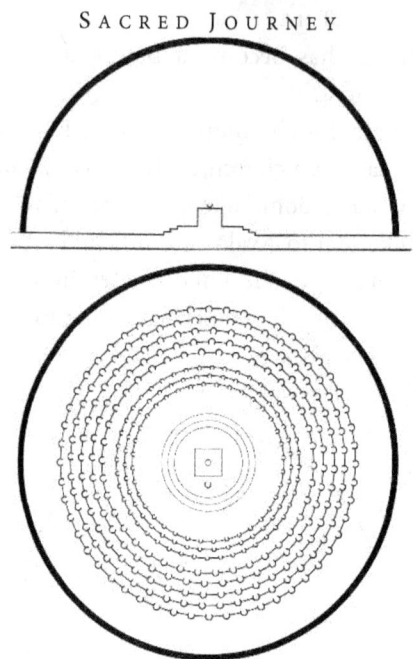

FIGURE 21. The First Plan in *The Church Incarnate*, page 37.

After presenting this plan Schwarz devotes twenty pages, from 39 to 59, to explaining it, saying (38, line 10) "Now we shall attempt to understand what actually happens in this form and the meaning of every detail." From a God-centered standpoint Schwarz looks down on the earth for whose surface he has proposed a series of structures, his Plans. For these he records the reactions of their congregations. For this book I have adopted a different standpoint from which to appreciate his work. By setting the Six Plans on a foundation of the six Christian ministries I am able to set out the six physical forms that will best serve those ministries. In our different ways we both wish to be of service to our fellow creatures: Rudolf Schwarz, a man of God, proposed various physical forms and observed how humans would react to them. I, from a worldly perspective, have proposed six ministries, and determined which physical forms would best serve them. The amazing thing is that our approaches, parallel but moving from different standpoints, seek the same goal.

In the passages that follow his illustration on page 37 Rudolf Schwarz wanders around his subject noting items of interest. He notes them as they occur to him, so they do not appear in any logical order. I'm not suggesting you don't accompany him on his journey—he discovers many beautiful things in his wanderings and reveals many cosmic relationships. What I am offering is not a map for that aspect of a journey, but a guide book. A map outlines a route, but a guide book merely lists what one might find. To that end I have abstracted six relationships (that number again!) which encompass the spatial experiences of a worshiper in a worship space formulated to serve the First Plan. Here's the list, referring to my simplified drawing for The First Plan:

First, the worshiper relates to the central altar where it marks a space for the sacred heart of the Body of Christ, his body and blood present in a loaf and a cup, and his countenance and word expressed in candlelight.

Second, the worshiper in his humanity reaches out to those next to him, his brothers and sisters who are within reach of his left and right hands, and by extension he reaches out to those who complete this ring of worship.

Third, he looks across the space and sees the faces of the whole gathering, all of whom are relating to their central purpose.

Fourth, he raises his eyes to the over-reaching dome, white and featureless, that offers no distraction from his appreciation of God's infinite presence.

Fifth, he is aware of the integrity and physical strength of the dome, preserving the security of the space and keeping it safe—this is the appropriate plan for the church where there is danger of persecution.

Sixth, he is aware of the floor. Although it appears flat it is an extension of the spherical surface of the earth that has its own dark center. In the buried chapels of the catacombs the darkness could extend over the entire dome, but God's light can still shine through that darkness.

These six personal relationships could offer a framework for Schwarz's reflections on this plan.

There is one factor that predicts the breakdown, or breaking-out, of this system: the presence of the priest. If the center is to be Christ then the priest has to be off-center. This establishes a unique axis, a direction, in a space that was formerly centri-symmetrical. It creates a connection with the totality of the outside world, just as the direction of the needle of a compass bespeaks the existence of its distant magnetic pole. It brings time into a timeless world. And the priest had need of a door to enter, which is also a door by which the people could leave. For a time we can ignore these thoughts and worship out-of-time in the ministry of Contemplation, but a time will come when we will have to again confront the world. Schwarz writes (65, line 9):

> "Our plan will not always remain as it is now—it contains germs of growth. These are still sunk deep into the centric pattern but they will grow tall and they will burst it asunder."

There are many Eastern religions with a focus on contemplation and meditation. Essentially these gatherings are not for worship but for experiencing the insights of private enlightenment. They seek individual experiences that are out of the body, out of space, and out of time. It is the Christ-presence that brings with it a responsibility for the well-being of his Father's world, and we find a sadness in our worship because we know that in that world there are some of our brothers and sisters who are not with us. Our altar might be surrounded by a glorious company of angels and archangels, the saints in glory and our beloved dead, but we know that the solid walls that are keeping us safe also keep others from being with us. This sadness motivates us to seek a way out of the dome's stony embrace; and the Christ who trod this path before gives us the strength to take it.

The Second Plan for the Ministry of Pastoral Care

This chapter could be the most difficult in the entire book, because it attempts to bridge the visionary concepts of Rudolf Schwarz and my interpretations of his insights, and as we are very different people with different approaches this puts a strain on language. You could, if you wish, regard this chapter as a bridge between his previous chapter and the one that follows—not that I would wish you to ignore or bypass Schwarz's writings. A bridge can make a direct connection, but it is not the only connection. You experience more of the countryside if you scramble down the bank, wade or swim across the river, and scale the cliff on the other side.

The problem that I have is that I am not able to enter, or even imagine, his God-centered Heaven-space. I'm just a man, standing with my feet on the earth, and by using earthly logic I have created a system of six ministries which generates a ring of six plans. These people-based worship-oriented plans may differ from the God-centered vision-inspired Six Plans of Rudolf Schwarz. We are in close agreement regarding our First Plans, you can see that our drawings of them are quite similar. That is because we are in agreement as long as God is presented as an over-arching presence. However, when we make a break in the ring we fly in opposite directions. And that is why the diagram for my Second Plan is so unlike any of the eleven diagrams he offers. To illustrate this I have chosen his drawing (see fig. 23) that come closest to mine. In *The Church Incarnate* it appears on page 74. Schwarz peels back from a split in the dome to create an opening which is a portal to Heaven, a token for an increased awareness of God's presence. In doing this, for Schwarz, the remains of the dome are mere shelter.

In contrast, I approach the Second Plan from the earthly standpoint of the People as an exemplar of their ministry of Pastoral Care. This ministry is defined by the parameters of the sacraments of healing, forgiveness, reconciliation, and care being offered to the people. As Schwarz writes (77, line 21):

"When the people come from their worldly ties to enter this church they experience their historical form as the form of ministering grace, for even the open and wounded form of this world is sacredly intended." (That is such a beautiful insight.)

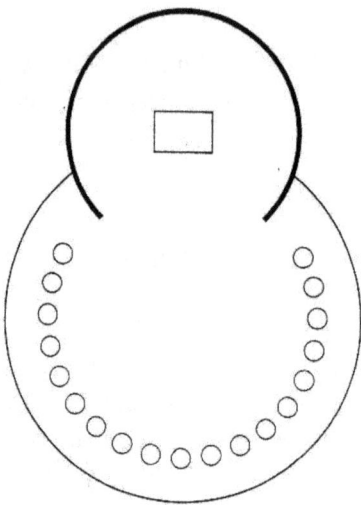

FIGURE 22. The Second Plan, for the ministry of Pastoral Care.

The First Plan created a sadness as the people realized that some of their brothers and sisters were still outside the dome and were still hurting. They were not able to receive the gifts of grace. Feeling this, in the Second Plan, although the people are still fragile and insecure, they open-up a possibility of access for others who may wish to join them. I have represented this in the diagram, not with a doorway (that would permit anybody to burst in) but with a thinner line that depicts a permeable wall, one that embodies a balance between access and security... so the space is still safe and contained while permitting entry to those who seek the gifts.

If I had wanted to name this Plan I would have called it "Sacred Meeting." It's not a sacred gathering because that implies that the people were selected for a purpose. It is not a sacred community because that would require membership and agreement. A meeting is just a temporary grouping of people who are free to come, stay or go, as they wish.

The two hemi-domes in my diagram, one solid and one permeable, reflect two qualities, perhaps contradictory qualities, of the space. The function of the solid dome is to keep the space safe, as it did in the original plan; and by its very strength to have a seamless surface, colorless and featureless, that allows us to project onto its emptiness a vision of the presence of God. The church is in the world, and the people realize that their hope and their destiny is to go out into this world, but that time is not yet. However they know that the gifts of the spirit are dedicated to all humanity, so those of their brothers and sisters who are still outside and wish to enter should be allowed to do so. To achieve this the other hemisphere has a permeable wall indicated by a thinner line weight. This wall acts as a filter to allow some individuals to enter but protects against any mass invasion, creating a fine balance between open-ness and security. It is built of ordinary earthly materials such as may be found in any builder's yard: glass block, automatic doors, outdoor lighting.

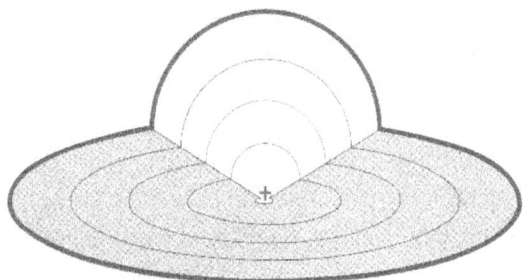

FIGURE 23. Schwarz's Second Plan in *The Church Incarnate*, page 74.

Schwarz approaches the Second Plan from a different place and in an opposite direction: he creates a large metaphorical opening by which God who surrounds and infuses everything outside may also be perceived by those who are inside—a vision of his Heaven. This opening is created, not of earthly materials, but in a brilliant fusion of glory and joy—it's awesome. The rest of the dome remains solid and protective, but by means of the opening the people see, for themselves, a possible destiny. The two intersecting domes create a single space, but the space has two qualities. It is the fusion of these qualities that creates a unity. The partial domes that together create a spatial boundary out of incomplete spheres complete one another. Each closes the opening in the other. Graphically they are represented by incomplete circles like the ones Schwarz uses in his diagrams to indicate the open-ness of the eye (page 16) and the focused attention of the individual. In this plan the individual forms come together in an embrace.

This brings into focus the difference between Schwarz's visionary Second Plan and mine. Schwarz's classification is based on the physicalness of his plans—in his First Plan the dome is solid and in his Second Plan it is split, but in both of them the ministry is of Contemplation, the people are just offered different channels for adoring their God. Schwarz calls his Second Plan (and also his Third) "Sacred Parting" (*Heiliger Aufbruch*) but that just refers to the openings in his domes—nobody leaves.

I am presenting my own edition of Six Plans, not to discredit Schwarz for whom I have great admiration, but to bring into focus his intent. Simply put, we are coming from different viewpoints: he from heavenly views of the physical world and I from physical views of the heavenly world. In my Second Plan the people receive the blessings of Pastoral Care which is a ministry quite different from Contemplation. In Contemplation one wishes to transcend the body and dissolve the world in order to become totally at one with the Lamb, while from Pastoral Care one is blessed to receive the creaturely gifts of healing, encouragement and support.

An important feature of this ministry is that the gifts have to be received in community: a personal enlightenment is not on offer. For this we need to be able to see one another, and Schwarz has outlined this network of communication in his drawing on page 41. His drawing shows a network of three hundred lines of communication, and that just from a single ring of twenty-five worshipers! However, a large object in the center of such a space could intercept many of those lines.

I have found in teaching a class that when we sit in a ring we generate the maximum of participation, but we need some sort of an object in the center of the ring to hold its center, because without it we would just be focusing on one another and not on the subject at hand. Over the years I have found that a low object such as a coffee table works best, perhaps supporting a couple of books, but definitely not a coffee-to-go.

Anything higher than such a table, such as a regular dining table, acts as an obstruction and gets in the way, and anything higher than that will cut off communication altogether. Also, if there are more than three rows of seating, those at the back will only be able to see the backs of the heads of those in front of them.

The Second Plan

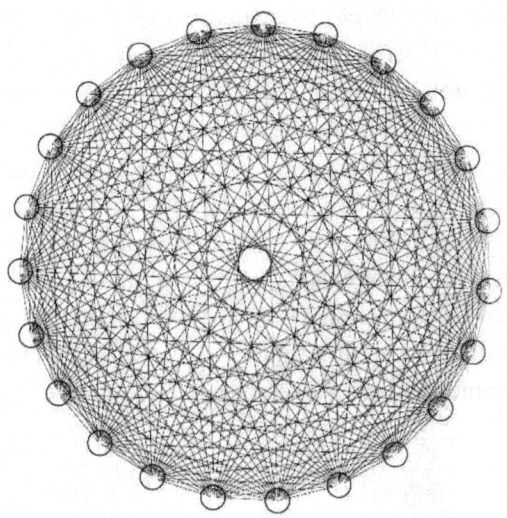

FIGURE 24. A network of communication from *The Church Incarnate*, page 41.

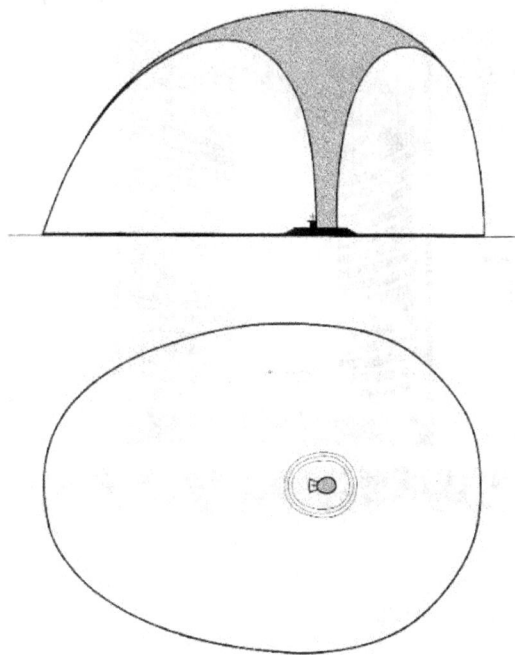

FIGURE 25. A church with a central pier, from *The Church Incarnate*, page 60.

Schwarz copes with this by raising up his altar on a central platform, but this creates the form of obstruction we have already noted. He seems not to regard this as a problem—in one of his plans the obstruction is a central column that rises and spreads over the roof. What he does not seem to realize is that by setting an opaque object at what was the center of the space he has created a new boundary to the space, and as the "center," by definition, has to be within the space, that center has to move to a new location, one halfway between a face of the column and the wall. The space is now transformed to the shape of a donut: a circular corridor with a curving center-line. A space like this is a very unpleasant place to be because within it one cannot find any sense of place.

FIGURE 26. Toronto City Hall.

There's a concrete example (forgive the pun) where you can experience this form of space in Toronto's New City Hall. This design for the building was selected in an international architectural competition in 1958—it was the

The Second Plan

winning design submitted by Viljo Revell, a Finnish architect. The design consisted of a pair of curving towers rising from a two story podium above which rose a clamshell of a council chamber. Much of the main floor level was to be "an indoor public square" out of respect for the Toronto winters, and the council chamber was supported above this by three sets of paired columns (six in all!) When the final construction drawings were completed it became apparent that the construction costs were going to exceed the budget. Outrageous! Unheard-of! Officials demanded economies.

FIGURE 27. Interior of Toronto City Hall. A central column obstructs the space.

One of the cost-cutting measures adopted was to replace the six columns supporting the council chamber with a single central concrete drum. This would be a more efficient use of concrete such as you can see in those sculptural concrete water towers which are shaped like a wineglass. This puts all the concrete in compression, which saves a bunch of reinforcing steel. So Toronto got a cheaper City Hall but its indoor public square became a circular corridor. The center of the space is no longer the center of the building; that has been occluded by a drum of concrete. Of course the space still has a center, but the center has now moved to a point mid-way between the face of the drum and the bounding partitions, the center-line of a wide curving corridor. This corridor is not a pleasant place to be, and nobody seems to enjoy being there. You can check it out. It's like the long walkway in the London Underground shown in fig. 15, page 20, except that unlike that corridor it has no destination, it just curves away around the corner and out of sight in both directions; curving away forever. There are many popular indoor meeting places in Toronto, but the City Hall is not one of them. That is ironic, because it is alleged that "Toronto" comes from the

Huron word that means "the meeting place." Schwartz attempted to sanctify his central column by building an altar into the side of it—in the same way Toronto attempted to deflect criticism by declaring the central drum to be a war memorial; that even though it contains the drains from the Members Lounge above.

For a church the central object should be kept low. If there are more than three rows of seats the outer rows beyond that should be banked, raised successively so everybody can see and be seen, rather than raise the central object. That object could be a communion table, or a low credence table bearing the water, bread and wine required in the Mass, or it could be a boulder or a floral display or a book on a stand, just something to anchor the center of the space. All this might sound a bit strange. That is because architectural schools are preoccupied with structure, and space is seldom mentioned or taught, and yet it is space rather than structure that generates the emotional response. Also, some could object to the prospect of raising some of the seating, saying that chairs on a flat floor gives maximum flexibility. True; but that flexibility could allow for a hundred different layouts, all of them wrong, while excluding the one right solution.

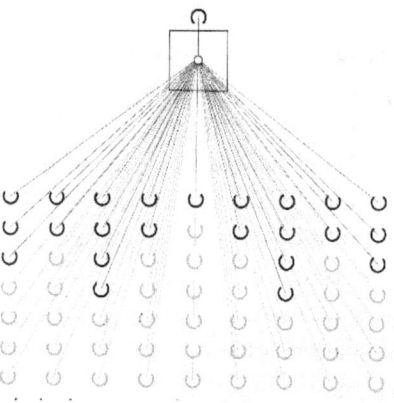

FIGURE 28. Seating for Seeing—not many have an uninterrupted view.

In his drawing on page 71 (fig. 28 above) Schwarz shows seven rows of worshipers with a visual connection to the altar. If they are on a flat floor the altar would have to be raised by eight feet for those in the back row to be able to see over the heads of those in front. This would be impressive—the altar of the Papal Basilica of St. Peter in the Vatican is elevated above the flat floor

The Second Plan

by only seven steps. However if the last four rows were elevated, each one just six inches above the one in front for a maximum of 24 inches everybody would be able to see. This is a very practical solution that I have advocated for many churches, where simple carpentry can produce the necessary platforms to support perimeter seating, and this gives an amphitheater effect which helps to focus attention. People should not have to put up with seating from which they cannot see. In figure 28 I have amended Schwarz's original drawing to indicate by a ghost image all those who would not be able to see if the floor were flat.

Schwarz sees a spiritual dimension to the world because the world is God's creation, so in approaching God one also approaches God's world. Thus the rent in his dome offers the people both an invitation to the presence of God and a possibility for leaving the dome to enter God's world. The people see this as a possibility but that is for a future time; they are still afraid. They do not yet have the desire, the courage, nor the resolve to leave their safe harbor, even though its safety is compromised by the split in its side, so its future is unsure. That is why there is a basic difference between the Schwarz version of the Second Plan and mine. Schwarz creates an opening in the physical dome so the people can enter a heavenly world, and I create an opening in the consciousness of the people so they can consider entering the physical world. In both these plans the space must remain safe, because for both of them the time for leaving is not yet. Schwarz spends the next twenty pages, 75 to 94, discussing this. Sometimes I have the feeling that he is at his most long-winded when he is least sure of himself. I respect and admire him as a wise mentor, so sometimes I lose sight of the fact that he wrote this work as a young man, and it was published when he was in his early forties. I am now much older than he was when he wrote the work, so perhaps I am also his mentor. In the foreword to the German edition Romano Guardini states "Newly created connections cannot be presented in full clarity immediately, and time must be allowed for discussions." Schwarz did not have a lot of time to create that clarity, he died relatively young at the age of 63, leaving a legacy of wisdom beyond his years.

The Second Plan, as I have presented it, comes into full flower in the Orthodox tradition. Here, the solid part of the enclosing dome, whose blank surface screens Heaven from earthly eyes, does itself become invisible and dissolves away, hidden from view by the screening of the iconostasis, so there is no visible barrier between our tiny church and Heaven; indeed the area holding the altar and screened by the iconostasis is itself called "Heaven." Heaven unites with Heaven, the Lord is with us, and tokens of his body and blood are brought out through the Holy Doors by his priesthood to share among his holy people.

So far, we have studied the first and second Plans as codified by Rudolf Schwarz. Both Plans embody the parameters of People and Sacrament, but in opposite directions. In the First Plan the structure is People-to-Sacrament: the community focuses on the altar. In the Second Plan the structure is Sacrament-to-People: the altar extends its beneficence over the community. These two Plans embrace all the possible relationships between a People and a Sacrament, and these relationships can be expressed as ministries that offer services for the worship of God.

However, for Christians, the world has a unique importance. Christians are required to embrace a duty to the World. That is an essential component of Christian ministry. Their worship must find expression in "works" as well as in faith. Jesus did not spend his brief time on earth worshiping with his disciples, he sent them out into the world. David Jenkins, Bishop of Durham, has said that of all the other-worldly religions Christianity is the most "this-worldly." This engagement with the world is expressed in the remaining four of the Six Plans (to be studied in the next four chapters) all of which are founded on ministries that have "World" as one of their parameters, thus enabling a congregation to enrich its ministry by extending its worship to embrace the world around it.

The Third Plan for the Ministry of Witness

Sometimes I wonder whether Schwarz lived in a spiritual world where all things contain their opposites. So many of the titles he gives his plans appear to run counter to their content. The title for his Third Plan: "*Heiliger Aufbruch (Der Lichte Kelch)*" is translated as "Sacred Parting (The Chalice of Light)"—this to describe a stone box with a hole in the roof! *Aufbruch* means departure or leaving, as does "Parting" (such sweet sorrow) but in Schwarz's Plan there is no way for anybody to leave, they are locked-in. In both languages these words have secondary meanings of a crack or break, but it's difficult to regard a crack or a break as sacred. I don't want to argue with my friend about which would be correct. I just accept that we are coming to the problem from different places. Rudolf is with God (perhaps literally as well as metaphorically) and both of them are looking down, while I am on earth, with the people, looking up. Thus Schwarz looks down on his model in which he has made an opening through which God can shine his light, and I am with the people inside it who are in darkness. We are blinded by a shaft of light, and we can't get out.

In the first ten pages of this chapter Schwarz discusses various historic structures that have solid walls supporting a solid dome. This dome could have an opening at the crown or a system of openings at the base to admit light to the interior. I have visited and experienced some of these interiors and my reaction to all of them is the same—they express darkness revealed by a shaft of light. Darkness is made visible; the overall effect is one of gloom. When I have had to deal with such an interior in re-purposing an existing church I have always advocated painting-over the skylight which was intended to lend sanctity to the altar, and to rely on "artificial" light which can be controlled. Natural light cannot be relied on—the unruly sunne keeps moving its beames off-target. This was well-known to the architects of the Middle Ages, so this design feature was seldom used, if ever, for a Christian church. There is evidence for this knowledge in Chartres Cathedral, where the south-facing stained glass window in the south transept has a small hole which admits a narrow beam of sunlight. As the world turns this beam rotates as it traverses across the floor in an arc which intersects with a brass stud embedded into the floor—but it only makes this contact for 1½ minutes once a year, at 12 noon local time, on June 21st.

These interiors featuring a shaft of light coming in from above give me a feeling of entombment, but there are exceptions. I don't get those feelings in the Round Room, a conference room in Massey College in Toronto. It has a glass roof so the effect is like being in a walled garden, open to the sky. The light does not enter in a single shaft, one is exposed to the entire firmament. Schwarz imagines a similar situation when he conceives of the space expanded hugely, to where (101, line 7) "an open valley lies beneath the sun and it is bordered far in the distance by a remote range of mountains." This could be a pleasant place to be, but it's a stretch to call this open space a chalice. His theology demands he return to his enclosing walls supporting a solid dome that is pierced to admit a shaft of light.

The prime example of such a space would be the Pantheon in Rome: a pagan temple built by the Emperor Hadrian in the year 126 AD. It is spanned by a 142-foot dome with a 30-foot opening at the top, which permits rain, and sometimes snow, to fall into the interior. Schwarz's illustration shows that its proportions were configured to exactly contain a sphere.

In 609 Pope Boniface IV consecrated the space as a Christian church, but its spooky quality remains. It led Dan Brown[16], the author of *The Da Vinci Code*, to include it as a venue of psychic significance in his romance, asserting that "The sixth century Venerable Bede once wrote that the hole in the Pantheon's roof had been bored by demons trying to escape the building when it was consecrated by Boniface IV." Other references to such evil presences include a narrative from an occult work:[17]

> "The garland of the trumpet was set afire, and then I saw the aperture of the dome open and a splendid arrow of fire shoot down through the tube of the trumpet and enter the lifeless body. The aperture then was closed again and the trumpet too was put away." and a warning[18] from *The Talmud*: "If the eye could see the demons that people the universe, life would be impossible."

---

16. Brown, *Angels and Demons*.

17. Andrae, *The Chemical Wedding of Christian Rosencreutz*.

18. *Talmud*, Berakhot 6.

The Third Plan

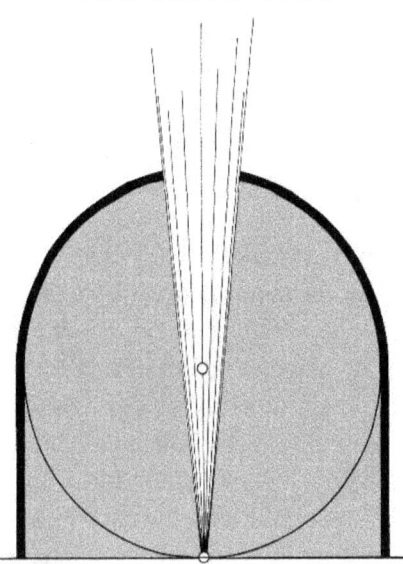

FIGURE 29. The Pantheon, Rome (*The Church Incarnate*, page 52.)

Clearly the Pope's exorcism was not entirely successful. His incantations did nothing to transform the space so it would be suitable for Christian worship. A dome with a large opening or oculus in the roof is not often found in Christian churches, and when it is so used it is usually for mausoleums and baptisteries. For mausoleums it can represent the broken tomb, with light streaming in from above. A similar image can be applied to baptism, represented as a symbolic drowning and rebirth. Cyril of Jerusalem[19] writes:

> "You were led to the holy pool of divine baptism as Christ taken down from the cross was laid in the tomb already prepared. You were plunged in the water and rose out of it."

The light streams down into the dome but none escapes, hence the chalice is dark. The people communicate only with the light. They raise their eyes to it in worship. They do not see one another, or anything of the world.

This form of building is used by many Eastern religions. Many temples, some famous ones, are constructed in this way. This form stresses the goal of personal enlightenment, a private path. It is a matter of indifference to the

---

19. Cyril of Jerusalem, *Mystagogical Catechesis*, II. 4.

enlightened that, outside, thousands are routinely dying in the street. This design could be appropriate for the various fundamentalist assemblies known as the Moral Majority. It expresses the goal of individual, personal salvation. The light streams down vertically from above. The walls of the dome are dark, in contrast to the blinding light from above. Our neighbors are dark. The world is a dark place, sinful and dangerous, full of perfumed temptations, illicit chemicals, and beckoning motels. The people too are dark and in shadow except for the minority that are standing in the light with us. And as the light grows ever brighter it may reveal darkness even in those closest to us. There is no one that can be trusted completely. The light can see everything. It is as brilliant as the studio lights shining down on TV Evangelists. It is as penetrating as the flash bulbs of the press, always waiting to expose our fall from grace . . . a fall for which there is no forgiveness, because once we enter or stumble into the dark we are totally cut off from the light. The dome receives light, but what it contains is darkness, and in this darkness we cannot see one another, so we are alone. There is no community in which we can join one another in worship.

Schwarz observes another physical property of the dome: its vertical axis marks out a particular point on the floor and gives it a special significance regardless of whether or not the dome has an opening. This can give an interior space a focal point, being an incident in a continuum, just as in a previous plan we noticed that a low table or similar object can give focus to a community gathering. He records this in a diagram (fig. 30) where we see an overhead dome giving importance to those attending an altar, rather than to the altar itself. That was the motivation of Sir Christopher Wren when he proposed a dome for his new St. Paul's Cathedral in 1666. This was at the beginning of the Age of Enlightenment when philosophy, politics, science and religion emerged from the authoritarian constraints of the Middle Ages into a new humanism. It was a time for new ideas. Sir Christopher set his dome not over the altar, not over the clergy, but over the center of the space where the people gather, claiming this sector of space for humanity as part of a new humanism.

A dome also has a presence at the exterior of the building. It proclaims that here is a place of worship, a function of the ministry of Witness which we will discuss later in this chapter. The rounded form of a dome proclaims heaviness, it's the same shape as a pile of stones, while the pointy slenderness

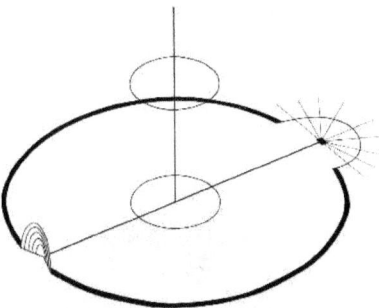

FIGURE 30. *The Church Incarnate*, page 110. A dome indicates centrality.

FIGURE 31. St. Paul's Cathedral, London.

of a pinnacle proclaims flight and lightness. In the same way the rounded form of a yarmulke or skull-cap implies burden while the points on the king's crown imply sovereignty. Sir Christopher neutralized the apparent heaviness of the dome by combining it with a pinnacle, setting a stone cupola over the dome to balance its downward weight with an upward thrust. I can't dismiss from my mind the image of a space rocket blasting off into the stratosphere, a narrow cylinder with its capsule of precious cargo atop a huge spreading dome of fire. This cupola, while proclaiming lightness, is itself a heavy object weighing about twelve tons—beyond the capacity of any dome to carry it. What to do? In earlier times a system of Gothic ribs would support it, but that would be visible from the inside, and would reveal the unacceptable symbolism of an obedient citizenry supporting authorities set over them.

FIGURE 32. A double-take at St. Paul's: the hidden structure revealed.

His solution can be seen in the accompanying cross-sectional view. Here we see that the weight of the cupola is supported by a conical brick structure which transfers the load to the foundations. The dome we see from the outside is a mere decorative shell, and another dome of painted lath and plaster hides the actual supporting structure, so the dome that we see from the outside is not the same dome as the one we see from the inside. Sir Christopher could have painted the underside of the dome sky-blue with flights of gilded angels swanning around in it, but that would be an illusion more appropriate to set over an altar. Instead he painted it with architectural motifs, as if it were a stone structure to shelter the people.

The Function of Schwarz's Third Plan

In his first two plans Schwarz created environments for worship which support the ministry of Contemplation where the People adore the Sacrament. Perhaps this is also true of his Third Plan, if any worship there is possible at all. Contemplation is the only available ministry for these plans because contemplation requires a separation from the world, and in these

The Third Plan

plans Schwarz has walled-off the world. The ministry of Pastoral Care requires that the people at least remember the world when they request relief from their worldly afflictions, and they allow other people of the world to join them in this request, but there is no mass exit from a safe space to enter into the world.

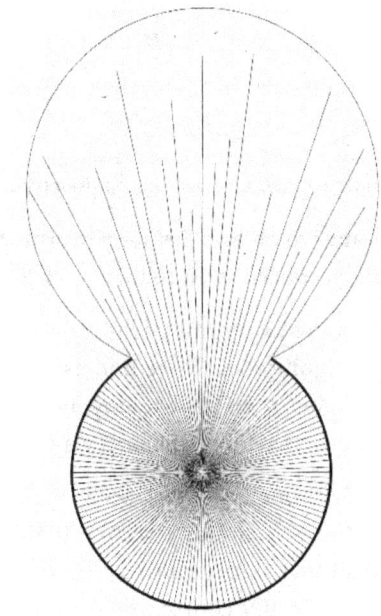

FIGURE 33. Schwarz's illustration for the Third Plan: *The Church Incarnate*, page 106.

Schwarz's drawing for his Third Plan, which is based on the Pantheon, is a vertical sequence of a people in an enclosed space looking up to the heavens. The opening does not allow them to ascend to Heaven, but they are able to witness it. This drawing depicts a hinge. A hinge is a connection between two entities, a door and a wall. A hinge allows the door to swing, but it does not change the door. It creates closed-ness where there was open-ness, and open-ness where there was closure. Perhaps the door remains still, and its relationship with the whole world swings on the hinge.

If we swing this plan around and lay it flat on the earth its structure remains the same but its relationships change. The plan now becomes "The Third Plan, for the Ministry of Witness" that was promised at the head of this chapter. The people now stand on a flat floor which is an extension of the surface of the earth.

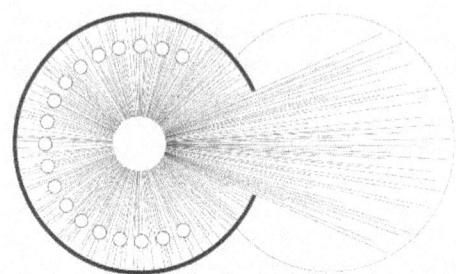

FIGURE 34. The Third Plan: rotated and laid flat on the ground.

The opening in the dome which was formerly overhead is now a wound in its side. Schwarz could have been open to this, (108, line 11) saying:

> "At the very last the two forms of the movement of opening would have the same significance. If we understand man in terms of his theological meaning, then the opening movement is the same both times, regardless of whether it seeks its way out forward or upward."

The light which formerly shone into the space is no longer blinding, so the people can see one another and in this community they can worship. Their worship generates a light that shines out into the world, replacing the light that was formerly shining in. Of course, the opening has just changed its position from the top to the side, but it has not changed its function. It never was a means for the people to rise up out of the dome so it has not now become a way for them to leave. It's a window unto the world, not a doorway.

The faint circular line which originally represented the Heavens now lies flat on the earth. It indicates that what emanates from the opening of the dome is not a random radiation but a beam of light targeted to earth-dwelling humans. It has a purpose: to proclaim the presence of Christ in God's world, and to invite and welcome the Stranger to join in worship.

The parameters for the ministry of Witness are "Sacrament-to-World." This relationship embodies the Sacrament being made available to the World. The people do not go out into the world. They have not yet found the courage to leave their safe place, but they feel a need to expand their horizon beyond their immediate community. In the previous ministry of Pastoral Care they allowed some members of their community to join them and receive the blessings of the sacraments. Now that the opening in the dome reveals that there is a world out there, they are moved to issue an invitation to the world to join them. Because they do not yet have the courage to go out into the world to present this invitation to the Stranger in person, all they can do is to advertise what is offered.

There are three ways they can do this. The most effective is to allow the world to witness their worship. A large opening, a window, allows the world to look into the space and see a worshiping congregation, and this could give rise to a wish to join them and participate in this worship. This is indicated graphically by showing the light generated by the worship of the sacrament shining out into the world.

Secondly, being able to view the interior from the outside at other times would reveal a worship space, and affirm that worship does indeed take place here . . . outside Toronto's Bloor Street United Church there is a sign proclaiming "It's Beautiful Inside."

Finally, creating a symbol could indicate a venue for worship. This could be a church tower, a spire, a cross, a statue, a sign, an internally-lit stained-glass window, or the sound of bells. Schwarz mentions (6, line 16) that in ancient times the gilded onion domes of the Russian churches were seen as holy flames, but they still inform us that this is a place of worship, as do the minarets for mosques. A caution: these symbolic expressions could be seen as invading public space, and among some people their effect could be more negative than positive.

This ministry of Witness, expressed in the Third Plan, can be seen as preparation for a great and terrifying step, a moving out into the world, a step which the Lord himself demanded of his people.

The Fourth Plan for the Ministry of Dedication

Sacred Journey was Schwarz's title for his Fourth Plan. I would like to consider myself as a companion to Schwarz on his journey, bearing in mind that companions do not always agree on the purpose or route for their journey. Schwarz seems to change his mind on these particulars, depending on what page he happens to be on. On page 114 (114, line 13) he says that this journey "leads from God to God" so it traverses a God-absent gulf, but on the next page (115, line 1) he says God will "be with them every day, up to the very end," and later he puts the whole journey inside the church (135, line 6) saying "The road begins with the portal and ends with the altar . . . The people stand between end and end and their standing consummates way."—so the people are standing, they are not moving. If you can stand the confusion, these multiple certainties are one of the things that gives his book its charm.

Up to now, a protective dome has sheltered the people of the world, but they remember the world they had left, and through a great window they are able to witness it. While experiencing this they have found the courage to consider going out into the world which was, and will be, their home. This is not an *Aufbruch*, the breaking of an opening in the dome to enable the people to depart. The dome itself just fades away, allowing the people to begin their sacred journey.

The people have been drawn together to gather around the Eucharist. This gave them the strength and courage to move into a new place with new challenges. The world which they remembered in the Second Plan, and which they witnessed in the Third Plan they now have the courage to explore. The Fourth Plan accommodates those who have embarked on a sacred journey of exploration. It also stands as a representation of that journey. It does not show the place they started from, that was entirely encompassed in a previous Plan. It does not show where they will arrive. That is in the future, not yet available to them.

The Fourth Plan

The parallels between the life of the people and a journey[20] was noted by Gerard Hughes, a Jesuit priest who undertook a pilgrimage from London to Rome in 1978. He observed:

> "On the road the pilgrim learns that searching for God is already to have found him, and that direction is much more important than destination, because God is not just an end, nor a beginning, but for us he is always a beginning without end."

For the people to be protected on this journey Schwarz proposes a new form of assembly, forming them into a tightly-bound group. Up to this point they have been meeting in a circle, worship-in-the-round, a form that was repeated in each version of the sheltering dome, and this form bespeaks an

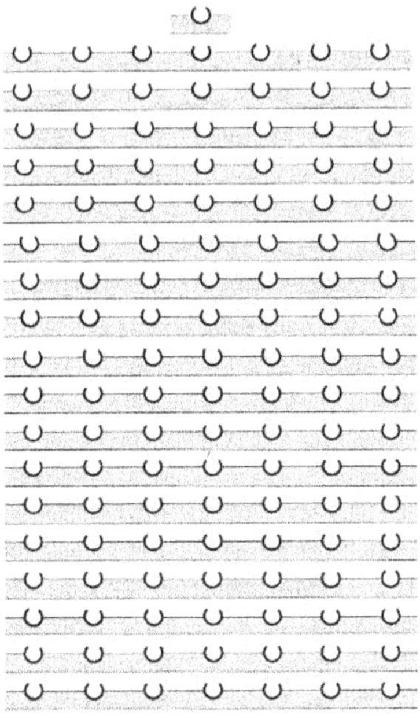

FIGURE 35. A military formation for worship: *The Church Incarnate*, page 129.

open-ness to a center. It is the form of a hand that is opened to receive, of arms preparing to embrace. Without the sheltering dome this form of assembly would leave the community vulnerable to intruders—they could

---

20. Hughes, *In Search of a Way*.

find themselves welcoming any intruder that came into their midst. The security offered by the structure of the dome they now have to find within themselves. Schwarz writes (and forgive the masculine imagery—it was written many years ago) (115, line 6):

> "In this marching army the men stand shoulder to shoulder, each man a link in a chain, each chain a rank. The next ranks stand a step ahead and a step behind, and many weave together into the order of the marching column."

This is the military formation adopted by a phalanx of Roman soldiers to defend themselves. When they came under attack by archers, on command, they would kneel down and hold their shields over their heads, holding their shields together, edge to edge, shield to shield, to create a solid carapace from beneath which they could hear overhead the ping of arrows striking metal—"shoulder-to-shoulder" also expresses a close relationship, a dedication to a common venture.

This is the most difficult chapter in Schwarz's book (and it is also the longest) but I would urge you to study at least the first seven pages, from page 114 to the top of page 120, because this is where Schwarz's humanity shines through. At times he can appear to be cool and aloof, creating models of structures to see how his subjects will react in them. The people are sometimes treated like those stock pictures of men and women that architects cut-and-paste into the foregrounds of drawings of their upcoming creations to give them "human scale" (and to help sell the idea of the project). In this passage Schwarz treats the people as real people, with all their individual complexities, and he senses the emotions that bind them together. In these pages he creates a linkage between the circular formations of the first three plans and the rectangular formation he presents for this plan. When we sit in a circle the center of the circle is where we focus our attention on God. When we assemble in the Fourth Plan, even though we do not face one another, we are physically closer to each other than in any other Plan. We all face forward, seeking a way ahead for us. That is our focus. Schwarz illustrates this transformation by gradually unwinding the circular form of assembly while the center point, the focus of our attention, gradually recedes. As the curve of the seating gradually straightens out the center point where we focus on God becomes more and more distant, until at the last the seating becomes straight, a rectangle, and all the sight-lines become parallel.

The Fourth Plan

Surely by making this final tiny adjustment we have not banished our Lord—he must still be at the end of every sight-line, so for each of us by facing forward we also face God. Schwarz goes into great detail in considering this formation. In mathematics there is a simpler way of putting it, without having to take apart the seating in the first three plans, by noting that in non-Euclidean space all parallel lines meet at infinity, the dwelling place of an infinite God.

After this Schwarz goes off on a side trip which he describes over the next fifteen pages, from page 120 to the top of page 134. On this great ramble he has many deep insights and sees many wonderful things. He wonders about chains and nets, additions and multiplications, sunrise and nightfall, drifting while on a voyage, the conflicts between tradition and progress. His prose is orderly. Each sentence follows logically the one that went before to create a continuous stream of consciousness, but the stream meanders all over the place, without direction. Meanwhile I am standing on the track where I await his return. But even when we are aligned on a purpose not everything is simple and straight-forward. At times the track is a dual-carriageway where Schwarz takes the high road and I take the low road. Essentially Schwarz, as an architect, is proposing designs for churches that will enable the worshipers to have an experience of Sacred Journey. My approach is to create a wayside chapel for a pilgrim people who are on that journey. At times I am presenting what is sometimes an alternate interpretation of Schwarz's insights. My hope is that this will focus attention on both possibilities.

Schwarz's proposal for a Plan (Fig. 36) shows an enclosure arching over the people. The form of this plan allows the people to have the experience of a procession, but its tunnel-form cuts-off the people from the world; although it was the people's impetus to experience the world that led to this journey in the first place.

Schwarz then adapts his Plan by creating a julienne of the roofing, slicing it into thin strips (fig. 37) This allows the people to see something of the world through the gaps. A careful study of this illustration shows that his plan has an end-wall; and the text reveals that (148, line 1) "an end is given the infinite road because it came to an end in Christ . . . Every design of a 'processional church' which sends the people on their way and brings this way to an end in the altar must rest upon it." If it is well-handled this end wall can become opaque to the eye but transparent to the spirit, but this

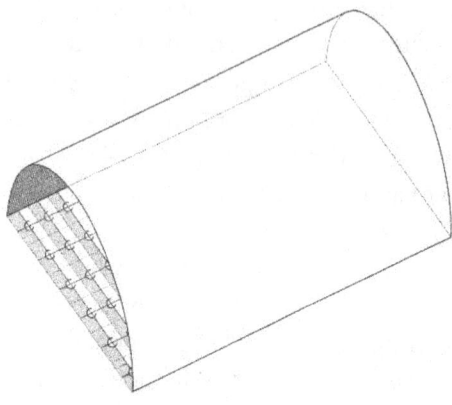

FIGURE 36. *The Church Incarnate*, page 137.

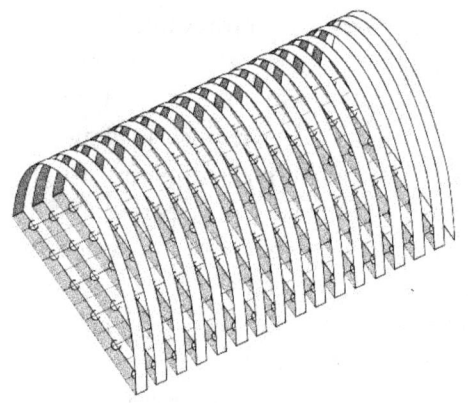

FIGURE 37. *The Church Incarnate*, page 138.

open-ness is negated if the journey is forced to end by an object such as a heavy stone altar. His concept for The Fourth Plan represents the end of the Journey, a spiritual home-coming.

As a church architect Schwarz had two clients: God and the Catholic Church. His designs for God are found in *Vom Bau der Kirche*; his designs for the Catholic Church are found in Germany. He was a devout Catholic and he bound himself to comply with his church's doctrines of the day, so with one exception he never had an opportunity to render any of his Six Plans into built form, in fact he expressly forbade it, saying (227, line 16):

The Fourth Plan

"The Plans... are genuine happening which has drawn utterly into its potentiality, which has become wholly seed and beginning and which waits, not to be copied down again, but to grow up once more as new event."

He felt he could not render any of his Six Plans into built form, or even allow them to influence his architectural work for the Church, so the buildings he has left us all embody a rectangular ordering of parallel pews with a central aisle leading to a raised altar. The only scope for creativity he allowed himself was in the enclosures he designed for this traditional relationship, as seen in his beautiful St. Fronleichnam Church in Aachen (see fig. 38, also illustrated on the front cover).

Here a pure whiteness informs all surfaces with a minimalist purity. The end wall is huge—as high as from earth to heaven, as wide as from east to west, without any distinguishing feature. Its surface is plain, seamless; nothing divides it—but when something is divided by nothing, as in x/0, the result is infinity. He notes (89, line 6):

> "We must be aware that the wall which remains empty here has something significant of its own to say, that it is not the termination of the altar but rather its unlocking and opening, and that for the whole building, too, it represents something utterly different from a simple back wall."

The featureless end wall dissolves itself. In drawing back its veil it reveals a distant horizon where earth meets heaven. That could indicate the possibility of another journey, but the barrier of an impassable holy mountain, ten-steps-high and supporting the high altar, tells us that at this time we cannot proceed further: that journey is not yet.

Schwarz designed the altar to be against the end wall, and when celebrating the mass the priest would face in the same direction as the people, as it was when he was leading them on their journey. Schwarz writes (78, line 2, and later 150, line 23):

> 'The priest goes forward to the altar as the representative of the people; there he stands erect facing the east, pushed to the boundary of the earth, the last man...
>
> "The whole people is on the Way and hence the priest should look forward just as all the people do."

FIGURE 38. St. Fronleichnam Church, Aachen. Beyond the altar the Way extends.

This powerful imagery evaporated when, after the death of Schwarz, the Second Vatican Council responded to the wishes of the Sixties Generation for the priest to face the people at all times. So a new small altar was moved forward and the priest was moved back. The priesthood lost their leadership role and became "just friends."

    It is ironic that three hundred years earlier, in the Savoy Conference of 1661, that was the issue that led to the separation of the Presbyterians from the Church of England. Twelve bishops and twelve Puritans met to debate on a new prayer book. The Puritans, who had a focus on preaching, held that the minister should face the people at all times. The Bishops said that the priest should face the people when he is speaking *to* them, but not necessarily when he is speaking *for* them. That prospect was too "catholic" for the Puritans so they left, and that schism remains to this day. Many wars causing thousands and thousands of deaths have sprung from such insignificant beginnings. If Schwarz had wanted the priest "to face the people at all times" he would have made the end wall a continuation of the side walls with the same high windows extending right round the end of the church to make a wrap-around effect, thus honoring the altar.

The Fourth Plan

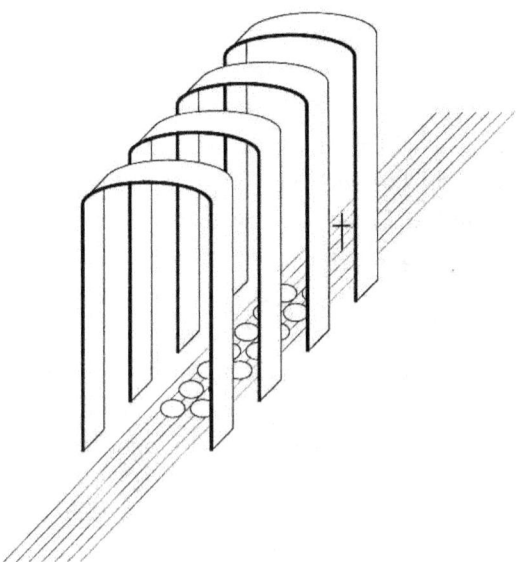

FIGURE 39. The Fourth Plan for the ministry of Dedication.

After examining the relationships inherit in worship I have created this Plan (fig. 39) for the fourth ministry, the Ministry of Dedication. The parameters for this ministry are World-to-People. The people leave their safe haven to experience the world. They are in the world but not of it. Their Plan is quite similar to Schwarz's Plan illustrated on page 138, (as depicted in fig. 37) except that his plan is for a church where worshipers can imagine they are on a journey, while my plan is for them to worship while on their journey. To this end, the structure is open at the ends and the pilgrim way extends beyond it, out from the past and on to the future. There is nothing to impede their progress. The fourth plan is linear: an arching over an open-ended pilgrim way. The people all face the same direction. They do not need to face one another because they knew they had become a community the moment they committed themselves to leave the security of their enclosing dome. Even though they do not face one another, they are in fact physically closer to one another than in any other Plan. They are held together by a common faith, and embarked together on a Sacred Journey. Their needs are few. They travel light, carrying a portable altar and following a processional cross. Their worship takes place on the road.

Sacred Journey

The Way is roofed, a vault arches over the roadway from one side to the other. This vault is not dark and heavy. Its purpose is not to withstand forces pressing in on the Way. In fact it is good if it can admit daylight so the people do not feel they have entered a tunnel. If the vault is built of alternately clear and solid sections, those moving through the space will experience alternating light and darkness, their lives measured out in nights and days. The ends of the enclosure need to be open. The Fourth Plan represents a stop on the Sacred Journey, it is not where the journey stops. We have to be able to see our way ahead. So at the ends of the space there should not be any barriers or heavy decoration that might obstruct or cause us to stumble. The end walls could be glass, so one could see a continuing of the Way, or a wall so totally blank it has no existence, or the ends could be a series of screens, to leave it ambiguous as to where the enclosure ends, so wherever we look, the end is somewhere else. The purpose of Sacred Journey is not a quest to reach God: Sacred Journey is a journey with God. The people have a processional cross and banners to proclaim their purpose. They carry their altar with them[21], as did the early Israelites.

Their worship is on the move, knowing they must press on. They know they will not live this minute again.

The differences between our two depictions of the Fourth Plan spring from our having differing concepts for "The Way." For Schwarz the Way is a spiritual journey that proceeds from a dark night of the soul to eternal bliss with the Lord, symbolized by an aisle connecting portal to altar. Nobody has to tread this track: the journey is imaginary. The people do not move. In fact they cannot move: the people fill his church to capacity. His church is so packed with people there is no space for anyone to move around—a nice problem to have! Looking at his illustration on page 137 we see that the journey has to be symbolic—moving would be impossible. They are packed in tight as if in a crowded air-raid shelter. On the other hand, for my church, the Way is a real journey through a real world. That is because for my version of the Fourth Plan "world" is one of the parameters of worship for the ministry of Dedication, the ministry that is the seed of this plan.

The Fourth Plan is supportive of those who are brought together for a short time for a common purpose, and who know that later they must

---

21. "Make poles of acacia wood for the altar ... so they will be on two sides of the altar when it is carried." Exodus 27:6.

The Fourth Plan

separate. It works well for the worship of schools and universities, where the goal is to equip oneself for a life in the world beyond. The ministry of Dedication finds its most extreme expression in monasteries and closed communities where a separate or private World has been created for the People, a world more perfect, without some of the temptations of the outside world, and for a community more perfect than can be found outside the walls. The Fourth Plan is also supportive of the worship of the business community, those whose labor in the World supports the worship of the People in an act of dedication. With great wisdom Pope John XXIII spoke of the whole church[22] as ". . . a pilgrim people of God. The church is seen as a Church of Pilgrimage to its true native land."

In this he implies that we should not overly burden ourselves with institutions and traditions, but rejoice in the freedom of the faith. Just as this faith has the power to continually restore and renew us, so must the church ever and always renew itself. We cannot rest on our laurels. Pope John also said[23]: "The Catholic Church is summoned to a continual reformation, she is the Church on her Pilgrim Way." We all have something to learn from Sacred Journey, because it is Sacred Journey that continually confronts us with something new. The Fourth Plan is the plan of Dedication.

In the last fifteen pages of this chapter, from page 139 to 153, Schwarz discusses various historic churches saying (139, line 5): "No other structural concept has so glorious a history as the 'sacred way.' In this connection we usually think of the medieval processional churches which unfold this idea with such magnificence." He goes into raptures over their dramatic beauty as their longitudinal form holds the Way in a loving embrace. However, as a former engineer, there is another thought lurking at the back of my mind. These medieval structures of stone and wood were limited in their ability to span space, so if it was desired to build a very large space, for a cathedral for instance, the only option was to make it of modest width but very long (207, line 3). Thus structural limitations forced the expression of a linear form. This created a need for processions. The long narrow spaces of many medieval churches required processions as a means of bringing the performers closer to the audience, at least for the brief moment when they

---

22. Reid, Vatican II, v.2, 20.

23. Reid, Vatican II, v.2, 42.

passed down the aisle. This form of space therefore encourages processional crosses, banners, thurifers, monstrances, vergers with maces, and all manner of portable sanctity. The great distances require chanting, intoning, and plainsong so the Word can be projected beyond the range of speech, and sanctus bells could communicate even further. Perhaps these traditions developed as a response to geometry: the measurement of the earth.

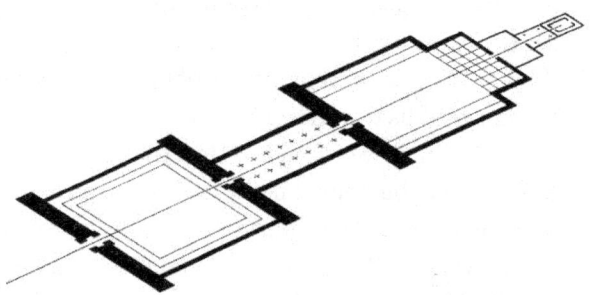

FIGURE 40. Interconnected rooms in *The Church Incarnate*, page 140.

For Schwarz a processional space is a space with a central aisle where the worshipers could imagine themselves in a procession. Such a procession is symbolic, whereas a pilgrimage is real, and takes place in the real world. He sees symbols of processions in those layouts which comprise a series of interconnected rooms. These are not pilgrimage spaces because they break up the Journey into stages where each one has to be completed before the next one can be undertaken. This is the format that could be used for a video game, or for the many stages of the journey of the soul[24] as listed in the Tibetan Book of the Dead.

Schwarz considers that this layout is a representation of a dark journey of the soul, a journey without hope, (140, line 7) while the pilgrims on a Sacred Journey are singing joyful hymns of expectation. We will be studying this historic plan more thoroughly in Part III.

In the final paragraph of this chapter (153, line 14) Schwarz deals with the urban church, and that we will be studying in Part IV.

24. Evans-Wentz, The Tibetan Book of the Dead.

The Fifth Plan for the Ministry of Evangelism

The title for Schwarz's Fourth Plan was Sacred Journey, a journey on the Way—a pilgrimage that finds its completion in the Fifth Plan. However we have different views of this pilgrimage. For Schwarz it is a symbolic journey "from portal to altar," a journey that takes place within the church and is a metaphor for "from confession to absolution" or "from baptism to communion."

By considering the worship of the church, which presents itself in Six Ministries, I have arrived at a different interpretation of the Fourth Plan. In my interpretation the Way extends beyond the church, and the church becomes an incident on that Journey.

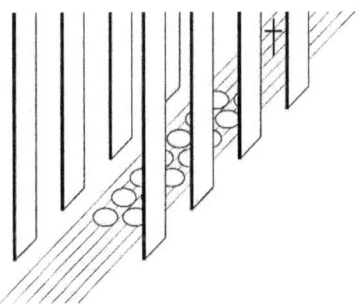

FIGURE 41. The pilgrims on a Sacred Journey approach the Fifth Plan.

Schwarz's journey takes place in the church, and mine takes place in the world. I have created a Fifth Plan (fig. 42) to illustrate this possibility by fusing a couple of Schwarz's drawings from pages 159 and 174; the one diagram resulting serves to illustrate both possibilities.

For Schwarz the Fifth Plan represents a refuge from the world, a world that is dark and dangerous. His outlook on to the world is so gloomy I can't help wondering if he was afflicted with a clinical depression. His self-description (88, line 24) as "an ascetic scaling the lonely peaks" bespeaks a life without much warmth or human contact. His times, too, conspired against him. He had lived through the horrors of the Great War, and at the time of writing he was witnessing the preparations for the next one. Even though it was his writings that gave me the impetus and the inspiration to discover the structure of the Six Ministries he might not have accepted my findings because they envisage the possibility of worship embracing the world—four of my Six Ministries have "world" as one of their parameters of worship—and for him the world is a place of darkness. As a source of illumination for this world he calls forth "star" (12, line 1) which implies a tiny pinprick of light in a sky of overall blackness. Thus he rejects the sun that warms us all over and sustains us. Indeed he calls this light-spreading church "The Dark Chalice."

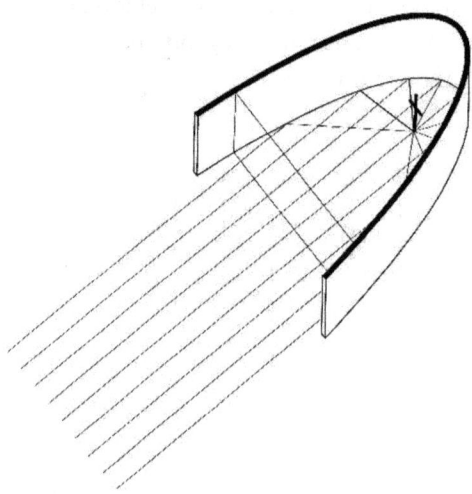

FIGURE 42. The Fifth Plan for the ministry of Evangelism.

In the opening lines of this chapter he describes how a people who are leaving their world for a new one are

> "... moving into the new land which has been made ready for them. They are coming out of the distance in a long train. Their journey is almost completed and now they are drawing close to the goal."

This sounds like a column of refugees seeking relief from the oppressions of a hostile land. At first the church welcomes them. The Lord awaits them with open arms, symbolized by the extending walls of the church that enfold

The Fifth Plan

them. He enfolds the people in his arms for a brief while, but then the time comes when the Lord must release them, for he too must die to the earth and when he can no longer hold them the people are forced to leave. The church is not to be the homeland the people desire; it's a transit camp from which they will be evicted and they will have to return to the world along that same darkened path (178, line 9):

> "That time of togetherness was only a passing episode in the whole course; heaven was touched for an instant and this touch was then taken along as food for the descent . . . In this form the light is not a blessed end and rest, but only the passing by of the Lord, a moment of blissful hovering in clarity, and then solace and succor on the way to the growing darkness."

In the five pages starting at page 160 Schwarz gives free rein to this despair. These are the most poignant pages in his entire book. He feels and expresses the hopelessness of those who stood with bowed head at the foot of the cross, their gathering darkness, the dreams abandoned and the feelings of loss that would resonate with the frustration he must have felt when the doctrines of his religion would not permit the realization of his theology in built form. We've been through so much together I wish I could give him comfort.

In contrast, in the first five pages of this chapter he takes on the role of architect. In these pages he records with admirable logic and clarity how his Fifth Plan (and mine) are bounded by a curving parabolic wall that expresses the flux of arriving and departing. He goes into careful detail to explain the parabola; how this always-inwards-curving but ever-spreading form indicates the possibility for an infinite extending of the space.

This parabolic space represents a culmination of The Way, and as we have different concepts for The Way we ascribe different functions to the space. For Schwarz The Way is the manifestation of a symbolic Journey that happens entirely within the space. He writes (176, line 15):

> "The people tread only the spatial part of this architectural work: that which lies between door and altar . . . The building must preserve this process in a standing form which carries out the movement inwardly."

This is a concept we have already dealt with. For me, The Way is a pilgrimage route, an alignment for a purposeful passing through the world. It is depicted as a route that was observed in the Third Plan, undertaken in the Fourth Plan, and now is reaching its destination in the Fifth Plan. The altar is set at the focal point of the parabolic wall. Lights on the altar reflect off this wall and become a beam that illuminates the Way. The people see the light when they are yet far off. The light shines down the Way which leads them to the altar where they experience the Lord's embrace. In this they become the light, and from the curving boundary of the Lord's embrace their light is reflected back down the Way. In fact, the Way is made of the light of those pilgrims who had previously trod it. A pilgrimage is not a journey to discover a Way, it is a way to discover a Journey that thousands have already trod through space and time.

The embrace of the Lord gives the people strength, but no embrace lasts forever. If it did it would be an entrapment. So the strength-giving embrace of the Lord must end, just as the suckling child must leave the breast, having gained the strength to become weaned and worldly. This is a joy—a different joy from the one of being supported: it is the joy of being a supporter of others which is the touchstone of the ministry of Evangelism.

The structure which Schwarz designed as a model for his Fifth Plan could also work for my formulation for the fifth of the Six Ministries. To reinterpret the model, it stands as a culmination of the pilgrim way—the culmination but not the terminus. The open doorway is the widest part of the church, implying a purpose of welcoming and bidding farewell, and the curved wall that holds the people in its arms implies both an embrace and a reversal of direction. Thus the ministry of Evangelism is celebrated, because this vast doorway implies a leaving, a going out into the world to make new friendships, but also returning with new friends, bringing a new harvest to the altar where they too will become missioners. Schwarz's proposed structure supports both these proposals. The people gather around the altar for the Mass, but the word "mass" is derived from *missio*: to send out. And over the west door he notes how in some churches there would be a huge rose window. Such a window would only work if the outside world were washed in bright sunlight that could illuminate the window, so such a window would bespeak the existence of a sunlit world. Such a window would do nothing for those for whom the world outside is a dark and dangerous place. Looking through this window to a darker world outside, all its reds and blues and oranges, all its brilliance, would be darkened to somber shades of gray.

The Fifth Plan

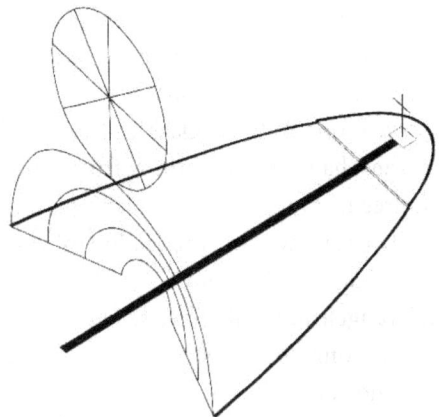

FIGURE 43. An illustration of a rose window over the west door (*The Church Incarnate*, page 157).

So we have two visions, or rather, a vision of two roles for the church: a sanctuary for protection from the world, or a beacon for those working in the world to bring new souls to Christ. Both are valid, noble purposes.

Forging a Plan

Neither of these two purposes motivated Fr. Wilhelm Eilers, who in 1956 was the force behind the building of a church in Bottrop, a coal-mining town in the Rhur, in northern Germany. Eilers had already read Schwarz's book and was familiar with his insights, so when he selected Rudolf Schwarz to be the architect for his church he also selected the Fifth Plan as his plan. Schwarz objected strongly to this misuse of his Plan which treated it as no more than a blueprint for construction, but it became obvious that the priest was determined to build such a church, with him or without him, so, unwillingly, Schwarz complied. So the church got built (see fig. 61, page 110) but for what purpose is unclear. In a town with a history of coal mining there was much experience of blackness, danger, and loss; and the dedication of the church to the Heilig Kreuz, or Holy Cross, could imply a congregational focus on Christ's last journey, a journey from the Last Supper to a crucifixion in a hostile world. There is no evidence that Fr. Eilers had any interest in

Evangelism, and indeed at that time I had not yet formulated the relationship between the Fifth Plan and that ministry, so why did he choose this plan, and argue so vehemently with his architect and his bishop to secure it? Probably because the structure itself is so attractive. It has such a minimalist appeal, enclosing space with just two walls: one of them straight and one of them curved, one of them glass and one of them stone. So the evidence is that the priest had learned nothing from *Vom Bau der Kirche*, he just used it as a resource from which to plunder a plan which would secure for him a notable structure whose implication of an infinite extension merely added to his self-aggrandizement.

An interest in Evangelism would have served him well. After an initial burst of enthusiasm the congregation steadily dwindled until it reached the point where it could no longer support the church, and the church was closed in 2008, fifty years after its consecration. Five years later, in 2013, a Sonderverein group took over the management, renaming it as Kulturkirche Heilig Kreuz e.V., or Holy Cross Church Art Center. It is ironic that it has fulfilled its destiny as a focus for Evangelism to an extent that would have been beyond the wildest dreams of its founders. Thousands of people now visit it every year— especially for the pub nights on a Saturday. It's a venue for recitals and readings, musical performances, art shows, choral groups and rock concerts. For the latter a newly-installed theatrical lighting system washes the walls in color. Schwarz might not have objected to this. Thinking of the future he wrote (197, line 27):

> "What the theater has begun could be further developed and the whole 'stage' for the act of worship could be set in motion. We possess the technical means for rendering such changing spaces of light."

To open up the space the pews have been moved to the sides. Marks on the floor indicate where they could be returned to their original positions if needed, and the church still has its Stations of the Cross on the wall and a large crucifix has a suspended sculpture of The Begging Christ, the work of Ewald Mataré. Who can tell what influence this might have on those visiting? . . . and over all, from the clerestory up above, a stained glass Eye of God looks down on God's children having fun in God's house.

The Sixth Plan
for the Ministry of Justice

This last of the Six Plans is the first one where Schwarz considers his work to be making a contribution to the World, and that only briefly. In discussing previous Plans he managed to keep the World at a distance, seeing it as a dark and hostile place, but for this Plan, which is totally open and there are no walls, he had no way to exclude it. Certainly he was justified in his rejection of what he perceived as the values of the world at that time—Germany in the 1930's was a playbook for overarching hate and wickedness.

His Sixth Plan has no walls, it is open to what he calls "Sacred Universe," but he has to take the rough with the smooth, and some aspects of the Universe are definitely not sacred. To cope with this he allows his worldly connection to exist only for the briefest instant, then the world reverts back to what he perceives as its former sinister role. I suspect Schwarz felt closer to God than he did to his fellow humans—God was a lot safer. The church building itself he sees as a House of God—God is the landlord and Schwarz is the tenant who is undertaking some renovations prior to moving in. I can't help conjuring up the image of God making plasticene models of toy churches, playing with them for a while, then squishing them back into a ball. He peoples his church with toy humans, made out of dust and breath. It was all in fun, but outside the nursery door the world waits, ominously.

Despite my respect, and even reverence, for Schwarz's genius, this play-acting was a formidable barrier to my understanding of Schwarz. Surely worship is more than just the acting-out of a static theological drama according to the rule-book of a doctrinal script? For my first eighteen years with Schwarz I struggled with this problem, then in 1975 I undertook to study what worship actually is. I was amazed at the way this played out—discovering that Christian worship is expressed in exactly six ministries, and each one is supported by the form of one of Rudolf Schwarz's Six Plans.

Schwarz would have found this troubling because the World is one of the parameters of worship for the ministries associated with four of the Six Plans, a World that Schwarz rejected, so suddenly there was a gulf between us, or rather a gulf between Schwarz's concept for a role for the Six Plans and mine. We were together for the First Plan that totally excludes the world, and also for our Sixth Plan which totally engages it, but between these two poles we diverge. This did not mean there was a gulf between Rudolf and myself—civil conversations are still possible between a Catholic and a Protestant, between a believer and an atheist, even between two architects. But there was no way to bridge this conceptual gulf, so I resolved to let the two concepts coexist, side-by-side. His concepts are certainly more beautiful and inspiring, more sacred and holy, than mine; but mine are more practical and useful, a role he expressly denied for his (227, line 25). Perhaps there is some value in two alternate concepts coexisting. Sharing our skills, I baked the cake and Schwarz iced it, so I provide the nourishment and he the image and the sweetness.

At six pages this is the shortest chapter in Schwarz's book, despite his title "Sacred Universe." He describes his Sixth Plan as "The Dome of Light," and much of his six pages is spent in a poetic discussion of the role of light. His translator gets caught up in this too. For this chapter she tends to get a bit flowery, translating "a light infinity" (180, line 14) (*eine licht Unendlichkeit*) as "a pellucid infinitude"—but why not?

The light spreads because his Sixth Plan does nothing to impede its sphere. This is the least substantial of all the six Plans. It could be realized, as he says, by a glass dome, or by a structure that is open all round, or by having no structure at all. Perhaps this formulation could work if the enclosing structure were so remote or irrelevant to the people that it would not enter their consciousness as any sort of a barrier between themselves and their vision of the world, so they could imagine their light shining out into the world unimpeded. Schwarz sees this Plan as an opposite pole to his First Plan where the people are totally enclosed in a dome that is solid and opaque. Perhaps he could have called this Plan "Sacred Outwardness." However, it was difficult for Schwarz to accept this effulgence as a flood of joy, of grace. From dark places in his soul the dark overtakes the light, so he allows the light to be only a brief flash in the darkness. It endures only as a memory of a promise of a future Heaven to those of us still struggling with existence on earth, saying (182, line 15) "This moment is ever a pledge of the other world which follows after ours."

There could be another more worldly interpretation of this Plan if we allow it to be an expression of the Sixth Ministry for which Justice is the touchstone, supporting equity, peace, freedom, and fulfillment for all. The ministry of Justice is the most extroverted of all the ministries in the cycle of

The Sixth Plan

worship. The parameters of worship for this ministry are "People-to-World": the people take the light of the Eucharist with them in their hearts and go out into the world, there to illuminate the world. Perhaps at some level Schwarz was aware of this, which could be revealed by studying his illustration for the Sixth Plan which appears on page 181.

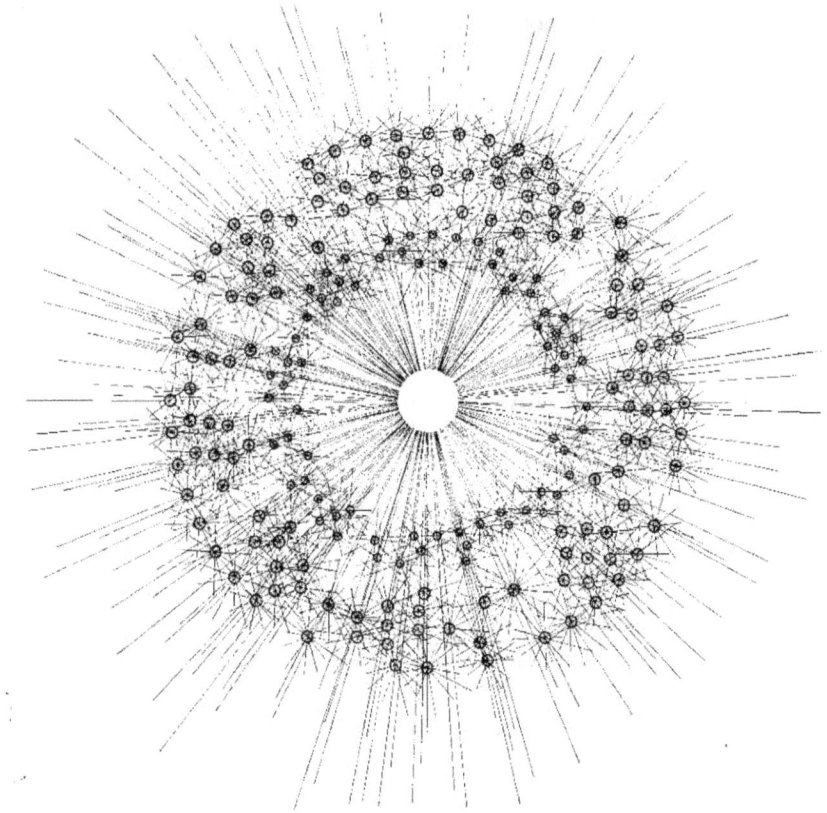

FIGURE 44. Schwarz's drawing for The Sixth Plan (page 181).

In this beautiful drawing over which he must have labored mightily we see the people represented as tiny sources of light. Tiny rays of light emerge from each member of the congregation as if they were tiny stars; as if each individual were a tiny fractal representation of the whole plan. And the people are not seen as seated in a ring, they are scattered in the space as if there is nothing to hold them in place, they are already leaving. They are going out into the world, each one a tiny church.

In his drawings for previous plans Schwarz depicted the individual people in his congregations by tiny circular arcs or cups such as we see in Fig. 35, and are similar to his diagram for The Eye on page 16. This indicated that the people were receptive, taking into themselves the blessings of the sacraments. Now the people are going out into the world to bestow those blessings on others. They are whole persons, which is indicated by their being represented by whole circles. They are now sources for blessings to bestow on others, indicated by the spreading rays emerging from each one of them. Could it be that Schwarz had an intuitive awareness of the significance of what he was drawing, but only at an unconscious level? . . . a prediction for the way his work might develop, or be developed by others? How else could he produce such a perfect illustration for a situation that he had not yet considered?

I am sure that the way he worked was first to draw all those radiating lines representing the spread of light. Then he would add circles depicting the people; 72 small circles on the three inner rings representing the children, and outboard of that 130 larger circles for the adults. Then, after many hours of work, came the moment of agony. His drawing was almost perfect, but it was still just a bit static, its execution did not quite match its inherent level of energy. The eye could tell that something was missing, but it could not say what it was. The Eye is receptive but the Hand is creative. This was a moment for the Hand to take over. Here was the moment of decision which would either fulfill or wreck his work. He was tired, and the decision was too hard to make, so he decided not to decide, to trust instinct, and let his hand draw the first line, the first tiny ray of light emerging from the heart of the first tiny person (any architect will be familiar with this process).

Having added a single ray to a single person, he then had to complete the process and add over a thousand more rays, distributing them to everybody else—that is the price of perfection.

PART III
The Seventh? Plan

Can there be such a thing as a Seventh Plan? or any Plan at all for that matter. What Schwarz calls his Plans are really proposals, ideas that focus on possibilities, so inherently there is no upper limit to their number. However, Schwarz, like myself and like most architects, is a visual person, so he cannot resist the temptation to sketch out some ideas of what these proposals would look like if they were implemented.

Figure 45. The addition to the Royal Ontario Museum looms over the sidewalk.

We can see what monsters may be born from such minimal conceptions when we note how a sketch on a napkin of a playful pointy structure generated the ugly angular addition to the Royal Ontario Museum in Toronto. This addition to a traditional masonry structure aggressively overhangs the sidewalk and dominates the passers-by—interesting in its inception but horrible in its execution. Not that Schwarz's sketches are ugly, they have stylish grace and are drafted with considerable skill, but we cannot avoid interpreting them as models for construction even if Schwarz expressly forbade our using them for this purpose. They concretize his ideas which then become doctrines, so we are tempted to regard the Six Plans as descriptions of six future realities. Can there be a Seventh Plan? Schwarz admits a difference between this plan and the other six. He presents his First Six Plans in Part II of his book but creates a special Part III for the Seventh. This distinction is carried through on the Contents page of both the German and the English editions, and I have adopted that format for the Contents page of this work, while adding a question-mark to indicate its questionable status. So the Seventh Plan does not just follow the Sixth Plan, it is a commentary and a sequel to all the previous Plans, just as the Seventh Day, a day of rest, was a sequel to all the previous Days of Creation. Schwarz's illustration on page 194 (see fig. 46) shows a Plan that borrows aspects from four of the previous Plans (numbers three, four, five, and six), not just the sixth Plan, so it is confusing for it to have been named the seventh. Perhaps "Plan B" would have been a better title.

The publishers of the English translation bear some responsibility for the confusion that surrounds this issue. On the flap of the dust jacket they disclose: "Schwarz discusses the seven possible plans for the church building." This is doubly in error. Not being set in the world the Seventh Plan is void of people so it has no application in the world, and as for the other six, Schwarz expressly forbade their use as building plans. He would have been appalled by this official-sounding pronouncement.

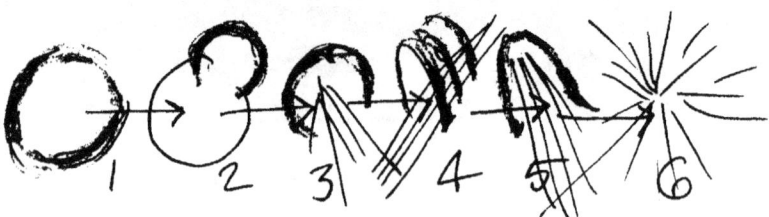

I think the problem arose when he set out the manifestations of his ideas in space and time. The people, as fearful of the world as I believe Schwarz to be, gather in his First Plan. By grace they gradually gain the courage to make baby-steps out of it into the next Plan that is slightly more open. This progression of his people through time is what links his first Six Plans. I've made a sketch, not as elegant as his, to illustrate this progression (above.)

The people move from the First Plan to the Second, and so on, until they all arrive at the final plan, the Sixth Plan. This causes the church of the

The Seventh? Plan

Sixth Plan to become hopelessly over-crowded, while leaving five empty churches in its wake; obviously an untenable outcome.

Schwarz's solution was to create a Seventh Plan: "The Cathedral of All Times: The Whole" (*Der Dom aller Zeiten - Das Ganze*). By being "for all times" it eliminates the concept of progression, and by representing "the whole" it eliminates the possibility of dedicating a particular space. This would be a great solution, except that, for us, it does not work! We humans, while on earth, are obliged to live in a series of particular here's and now's. Time for us is an ever-rolling stream whose flow we cannot dam up nor reverse, and if we are "here" we cannot be "there." So this concept does nothing to solve the problem for his people. Perhaps beyond space and outside time this church could exist in Heaven; but a church is hardly needed

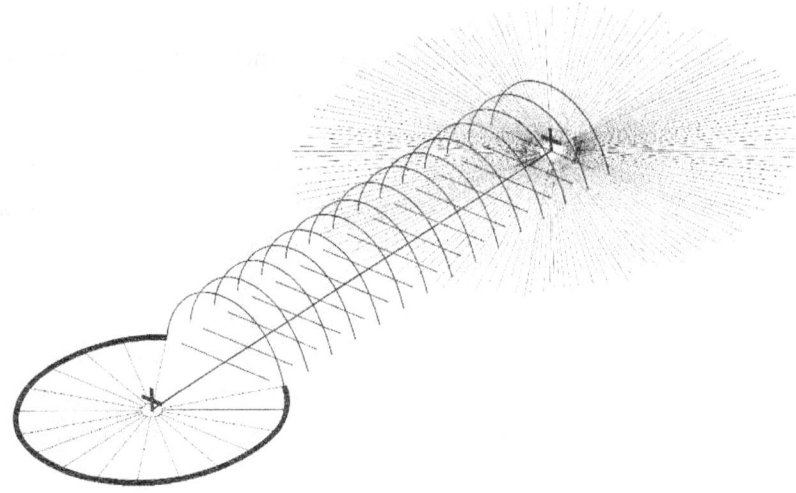

FIGURE 46. Schwarz's illustration for The Seventh Plan (page 194).

in Heaven because the whole of the Heavenly City is already a place of worship.

The appearance of Schwarz's Seventh Plan on page 194 follows the sequence of my diagram on page 77, but much more elegantly. However it embodies a different interpretation of the role of the arrows. In my plan they indicate a progression through time, and this is supported in Romano Guardini's foreword[25] to the German edition, where he says:

> "The illustrations of the church are not based on concepts of construction but of a living happening. "Church" here is presented as a process passing through world-time. The architectural forms of church appear . . . as great clarifications of that mysterious procession in which the people of God travel through time."

However this is negated for the Seventh Plan where the Plans are presented as elements of a new single Plan that exists in space. With this diagram, together with the name he gives it, Schwarz attempts to unite all six Plans into a single form. However Schwarz has given each of his Six Plans a name, and Spencer-Brown[26] in his *Laws of Form* states that "calling a name makes a distinction," and such a distinction creates a boundary (Spencer-Brown: Chapter 1.) That boundary is preserved even when these forms are nested inside another form (Spencer-Brown: Chapter 6) so creating an overall Plan to contain the Six Plans does not eliminate the boundaries between them. It is possible to cross a boundary to enter one of the Plans, but to enter an adjacent form it would be necessary to cross that boundary again, and Spencer-Brown's Axiom 2 states "for any boundary, to recross is not to cross." Schwarz's nesting of six Plans inside a seventh does not make them concurrently accessible to a single congregation any more than six separate churches in a city would be. The effect of the Seventh Plan is to have no effect.

Schwarz's concept for his Seventh Plan shows all six Plans co-existing, joined end-to-end into a single arcade structure where one may wander from Plan to Plan as if in a department store. Where is God in this? And what commitment binds the people to create such a structure? In fact the idea behind this Plan deconstructs the idea of the church as a body and turns a worshiping people into separated individuals.

Schwarz's Seventh Plan is a model of deconstruction. I can visualize models of his first Six Plans, but his Seventh is so ephemeral I find it impossible to imagine a physical image for it. Its form is so multivalent it is not able to convey a spiritual meaning—its parts are in conflict with one

---

25. Guardini, Foreword to *Vom Bau der Kirche*.

26. Spencer-Brown, *Laws of Form*, ch 1, ch 6.

The Seventh? Plan

another. Those who find a value in the Seventh Plan, or those who equate it to the other Plans, must be unaware of the incomparably greater value and purpose inherent in the first Six. Perhaps the kindest thing that can be said about his Seventh Plan is its implication that people should have the option of worshiping God in different ways at different times.

The internal contradiction in the concept is revealed by comparing two descriptions (191, line 15 and 193, line 31). In the one:

> "A single movement flows uninterruptedly through all the "plans" and one of its bases is set down in each of them."

> and in a description for his Seventh Plan: "that building which summons all phases into structure at once."

So Schwarz copes with the effects of a migration of people through his Six Plans by creating a Seventh in which they can be redistributed. To do this he had to fuse the spaces of his Six Plans into a single space that exists outside of space and time; a concept which offers no support at all to the church here on earth. This is a dilemma. My solution to this problem is to base a coupling of each of the Six Plans to a ministry it supports.

We have seen in our first chapter that there can be no more than six ministries so we know that there can be no more than six distinct Plans. In the sixth ministry, when the people have gone out into the world they have left their safe haven and are exposed to danger. They have to carry within themselves the security of the faith. Inwardly the People have to embody the Sacrament, which is the relationship of the first ministry: the ministry of Contemplation. Thus the sixth ministry creates the need for the first ministry, creating a ring.

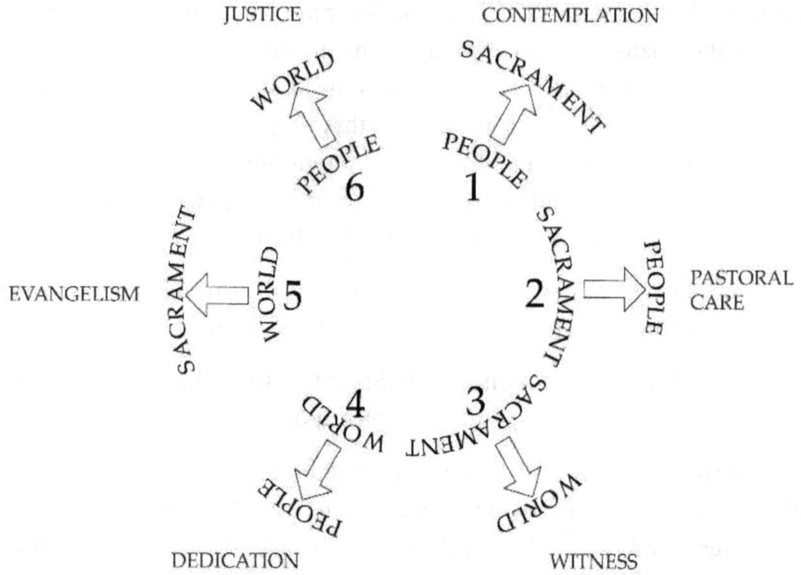

SACRED JOURNEY

JUSTICE   CONTEMPLATION

EVANGELISM   PASTORAL CARE

DEDICATION   WITNESS

FIGURE 47. The Cycle of Worship, showing the six possible relationships between pairs of parameters of worship, and outboard of them names for the six ministries they generate. Numerals indicate the corresponding Six Plans.

This means that we can also set the Six Plans in a circular array, as Plans and ministries are coupled together, and this array is complete, revealing that because there is no seventh ministry there is no need for a Seventh Plan. However the order of ministries in the array relates just to the way they were formed. Having been formed, they may be experienced in any order. The liturgy for any service probably contains expressions of several ministries and these could occur in any order. Indeed the six petitions in the Lord's Prayer are expressions of all six ministries, and this prayer can be offered in any of the six Plans.

The reason why I have expounded on the structure of Schwarz's concept of a Seventh Plan in such detail is because although the Seventh Plan is ineffective in itself it could lead to unfortunate outcomes. The Seventh Plan attempts to combine Plans based on several ministries into the same space. In the real world I have found this to have a profoundly negative effect. After visiting and studying over a thousand churches I have come to the conclusion that when a worship space is aligned with one of the Six Plans it evokes feelings of peace, calm, purposefulness, and integrity. When we

The Seventh? Plan

visit a place of worship whose planning is not based on a ministry, or is based on aspects of several different ministries, we find confusion and irritation. It is as if we cannot find a *gestalt* for the place; we cannot understand it; it has no sense of wholeness, it sends us mixed messages. In attempting to get our heads around such a space we expend energy and experience a confusion which makes worship difficult. So it is of vital importance for a community to select one of the Six Plans as a guiding principle for configuring the physical form of its worship space.

One of the frustrating yet endearing qualities in his wonderful work is the way Schwarz develops a concept and then when it is almost complete he drops it and takes off in another direction. He's ahead of the pack and the finish line is in sight. We are cheering him on, and just before crossing the line he changes his mind and goes off somewhere else, as if he is suddenly struck by the enormity of what he is undertaking. How could he not see in his drawing for the Sixth Plan (fig. 44) that he was making a hundred and two miniature drawings of the First Plan? And on several occasions (191, line 31, and page 193, line 7) he likens the succession of Plans to stages in the growth of a plant starting with a seed that germinates, sends forth a shoot, and grows a blossom, but he never gets to the point where he says that the purpose of the blossom is to create new seeds, to start the beginning of a new cycle that will make new plants. His foundation is Catholic doctrine: a linear progression of cause-and-effect, as opposed to recursive doctrines such as those that are found in some Eastern religions. For Schwarz nothing doubles back on itself in a ring of re-creation. Everything runs in a straight line which, if continued, could lead to an inevitable and terrifying end. Indeed he almost gets to the point of supporting my approach of basing the succession of forms on the six ministries of worship, saying (198, line 1):

> "It is conceivable that in the future our churches may come into being solely out of the act of worship itself!" (Disclosure Statement: Apologies, but I could not resist adding the exclamation mark.)

This chapter is by far the most complicated in his entire book, describing with admirable precision the lineaments of a form that cannot exist. Fifteen pages are devoted to this, in writing whose beauty is unsurpassed. Schwarz creates a history out of time. His logic is spiritual, his focus wide-ranging. He writes (190, line 4):

> "These plans were founded in grace, which renews the dissolving forms, and therefore they were made whole in God who closes the gaping form . . . The world was placed in the landscape of eternity where the great eternal movement flowed through it and the sight of the eternal places gave it direction. The natural form of the universe was the bearer of an eternal meaning."

Temperamentally he was a bit of an antiquarian, finding evidence of this eternal meaning in his study of many historical structures, including, on page 202, a sensitive analysis of the churches of the Eastern Communion. His interest in these was understandable because at the time of writing they surrounded him on all sides. There were very few "modern" buildings for him to experience. That was his environment, so it was wonderful that he could achieve such a stripped-down clarity in his own work, where, in the last five pages of this chapter Schwarz comes down to earth and shares with us his comments on the interpenetration of "process and lastingness" (*Vorgang und Dauer,* literally "process and duration" but could be more aptly translated as "the temporal and the eternal") in some of the interactions he has had in his career as an architect.

PART IV
The Test

Although "The Test" is a possible translation of *Bewährung*, the title of Schwarz's final chapter, I'm not sure that this translation catches his intent. In the academic world we have lots of tests. These tests are to assess the knowledge and skill of the proponent. In that regard, they are looking backwards, assessing what has been done. In contrast, *Bewährung* has forward-looking overtones of fitness-for-purpose or probation which are oriented to ability in a future performance, and I think it is in this sense that Schwarz heads up his final chapter. I think the purpose of his final chapter is to secure for his book the role of being a valuable influence in the world—and that goes for my final chapter too.

However Schwarz's work and my work have different purposes. Schwarz wrote in *Vom Bau der Kirche* (31, line 9) that his book was "a collection of thoughts that occurred to us about our own work," and its purpose was to reveal the spiritual basis of architecture so a church building might become a fitting House of God. My purpose is to make Schwarz's writings more accessible, to clarify his concepts, to set them in a useful logical framework, and to reveal how these concepts have been of real value to the congregations I have worked with during my career as a Liturgical Consultant: and that in the hope that others may benefit from them. These purposes are quite different. Our plans require different tests to establish their value. Schwarz's physical Plans require spiritual validation, and my theological plans require evidence of their practical value. I was surprised by what appeared to be a reversal of our roles until I discovered a precedent that establishes value for both in the *Tao Te Ching*[27] of Lao Tzu, a philosopher of the sixth century BC (The following translation is from Roland Barthes' *The Responsibility of Forms*).

---

27. Barthes, *The Responsibility of Forms*, 194.

"Being offers possibilities, it is by non-being that one makes use of them."

This sentence neatly states that the physical gives rise to our contemplations but it is their spiritual quality of non-being (or not-yet-being) that enables them to become manifest. Thus Schwarz's six model Plans provided for me the inspiration with which to order the worship of real churches in the real world.

Schwarz has provided us with a whole series of designs for architectural models of imaginary churches. Despite his commandment that they are not to be constructed or copied, saying (227, line 11): "These things must change utterly into their potentiality if they are to grow up once more as something new." What we hold in our minds as we consider his Plans is a collection of miniature models of churches; spiritual dolls houses if you wish. We think about these models as being real and physical even though they could not be built, because that is the way we remember them as concepts, that is the way we hold them in our minds, analyze their features, and assess their value. For Schwarz, that assessment of value is "The Test" which forms the last chapter of his work. On the other hand, my six plans are spiritual: they are expressions of worship based on the six ministries of the Christian church—perhaps I should not have called them "plans," but I did. For me The Test is to see if these spiritual concepts can have practical application. I'll deal first with Schwarz's approach in "Testing the spiritual value of the Six Plans," then with mine in "Testing the practical value of the Six Ministries," and hopefully we can end up close by, if not in the same place.

Testing the Spiritual Value of the Six Plans

One of the difficulties with Schwarz's writing lies not with what he writes, but with "why." What's he getting at? . . . and by the time we've got that problem figured out he's off somewhere else. His wanderings make it difficult for us to find a context for his work, but they do enable him to access all sorts of other concepts, an enrichment that would not be available if his work were strictly linear.

Among the many themes Schwarz investigates in this chapter I have identified three. They crop up here and there, seemingly at random, so to provide a context I'm gathering up some of his thoughts into these three categories:

The Test

The function of a book (including this one,)

The role of the architect or builder, and

Our duty to God.

These will serve as the basis for the Test. The Test (for Schwarz) is how his book is able to serve the architect or builder, and how the work of the architect or builder will be able to serve God.

The Function of a Book (including this one)

Right off, Schwarz announces (211, line 3) that his book "is intended to be a primer for church building—no more, but also no less." Perhaps the English translation here is more accurate than the original German: "*ein Lehrbuch*" is simply a textbook, but "primer" implies a small introductory schoolbook, a basic manual of instruction that starts from the simplest beginnings. This is a good description of *The Church Incarnate* which starts with the spirit and ends with the stones, leaving it to others to make scholarly interpretations.

The Church Incarnate is a book about architecture; about building. In my entire career as an architect I have never purchased a book on architecture that was of any use at all—except for the 1938 German edition of *Vom Bau der Kirche* (My *Church Incarnate* does not count; it was a review copy). My copy of the German edition is over eighty years old. It's quite fragile and showing signs of wear. The pages have turned sepia brown, and their heavy dense Germanic type is getting hard to read, but still his wonderful drawings shine out like gems in a dusky setting. The problem I personally have with books is that before making a purchase I have this inner debate with myself to decide whether I should choose it, so it follows that I select only those books whose value is predictable, and that ensures that they will contain little that is new. The valuable books are ones that presented themselves unasked: the gifts, the ones I picked up in a yard sale or found lying about or that somehow dropped into my life. The Apocrypha from which I quote The Epistle of Barnabas on page 8 I picked out of the garbage outside the Church of St. George the Martyr. Otherwise, books that have had some usefulness in architecture would be books on other subjects; on astronomy, theater, mathematics, quantum theory, poetry, therapy, chaos, and alchemy; and in those cases their usefulness to architecture was a surprise. To select for us what would be that perfect book the Library Angel needs a whole library as a resource to choose from.

Schwarz asks (216, line 1): "Can there even be such a thing as a book that teaches doing?" This question could have a Y/N answer, but you would have to read the rest of his chapter to find out which one. He classifies his own book as "instructions about building" but he is careful to define and limit its role. With admirable precision he writes (219, line 3):

> "With the 'plans' we introduce something new into the doctrines of architecture and we must contrast the new with the known lest they be confused. First of all, our 'instructions' are not model designs; secondly they are not specifications; thirdly they are not parts of an architectural 'canon'; and, fourthly they are not 'formulas'."

He has already cautioned at length about not regarding his "plans" as model designs; here he expounds at length over the next six pages, 219 to 224, on the remaining categories.

In the *Specifications* section, page 219, he denies the attaching of a description of any physical reality to his "Plans."

In the *Canon* section, page 220, he denies the indulgence of using a mystical doctrine to order the form of a building, whether this be based on sacred dimensions, number theory, geometry, literary metaphors, or indications of an esoteric significance.

In the *Formula* section, page 221, he warns against "method without content"—adhering to doctrines which prevent the church from once more arising as new.

It's really unfortunate that at the end of this section (224, lines 13–28) he missed out on an opportunity to expound on the role of space—unfortunate but understandable. He was so preoccupied with wonder at the new possibilities that the 1920's opened up with new materials and new methods of construction he was deflected from considering the importance of the opposite reality, that of space itself; although its influence remained a factor in his unconscious. He refers to the duality of space-and-object as "surface-and-content," and his take on "content" is that it is accidental, it is whatever happens to be limited and defined by surfaces. In fact he has a high regard for shell construction, because here the outer surface obediently follows the inner and the form of the interior space can be apprehended (but not experienced) from the outside, or from above in a God's-eye view. The ultimate departure from this inner-outer identity would be the Catacombs, those underground chapels where the inner surface defines a tiny cave as "content," while the outer surface is that of the entire sphere of the Earth. Of course in his built work Schwarz was sensitive to the implications of space, he was a master in that regard, but it was always in response to intuitive promptings. He never revealed how these instincts sprang from a conscious purpose. Here we come up against what a book can teach and what is beyond its capability. (214, line 31) "This is the reason why our literature bears so little fruit: . . . the words of the builder are lacking in it." But the two of us are builders, so perhaps this will help.

The Role of the Architect/Builder

Schwarz reflects that:

> "Building is one of the true callings, one of those that asks the ultimate questions and whose work is total. The architect who builds is the governor (my preferred translation of *Statthalter*) of all architectural reality. He gives visible form to that which erects itself secretly inside of men" (212, line 31). When it is well done church building is "work which prays" (212, line 15).

Here we are in strange agreement. In our first chapter, The Foundation, we learned (on page 19) that "space is described in terms of our bodies . . . it may be expressed as a verb: it can dance, it can sing, and it can worship," and with this capability it can accompany and support a congregation in its worship. Schwarz gives the congregation itself a spatial configuration, like the "content" we mentioned earlier, saying (228, line 24):

> "The congregation . . . is not a formless mass, a filling liquid, rather is it elemental form, and its structural measure corresponds to that of the individual body so that it too may be called sacred body."

This gives the architect an obligation to link the prayerfulness of the space with the devotions of the congregation by building a place to serve this unity. This is a heavy responsibility. Architecture makes the heaviest demands of all the professions. If I should walk through the university campus in the middle of the night all is in darkness—the Arts students are all having sweet dreams and the Engineers are out somewhere carousing, but the School of

Architecture is ablaze with light as the students attempt to create a perfection for themselves out of themselves. The Architect (213, line 28) "constantly gives his very self to his works, he gives himself away." This sacrifice is a heavy burden that must be joyfully borne. Sometimes a young person has asked me about how to become an architect (because they are good at drawing). I try to discourage them, telling them that this is a dangerous addiction which they should avoid if possible; but if that is not possible, then Good Luck!

Schwarz notes that the Architect's whole hope is "that many of his works will turn out well." To quote Sir Henry Wotton[28]:

> "Well-building hath three conditions. Commodity, Firmnesse, and Delight."

In this he was translating a phrase he admired from Vitruvius' 15 BC *de Architectura*: "Firmitas, Utilitas et Venustas." "Commodity" means fitness-for-purpose, and for a church that means "fitness for the worship of God," "Firmnesse" means structural strength and integrity, and "Delight" means eliciting feelings of joy, hope and gratitude. It is the human response of delight which distinguishes architecture from building; so our churches should inspire delight. Schwarz comments that the building art (229, line 14) "erects the felicitous moment to lastingness, deposits the infinite joy in great forms."

Our Duty to God

We may do our best to build a church for the worship of God, but we know that in this we cannot succeed. The perfect church cannot be created because a perfect church demands a perfect world, and a perfect world must wait for the return of Christ, when the world will become God's world and we will become God's people. While we wait, all we can do is to do our best, in the full knowledge that this is not enough, that we are falling short. But we are not permitted to despair. That would invalidate our sacrifice which must be offered-up joyfully. *Non Nobis*—it's not to us but to you, O Lord, belongs the glory. To us belongs a duty which is an honor for us to undertake. We undertake this task with the hope of success as our guide, and

---

28. Wotton, *The Elements of Architecture*.

the knowledge of our inevitable failure as the expected outcome; what Schwarz calls, on his last page (231, line 18) "true and sacred failure."

Testing the Practical Support for the Six Ministries

For me, the Test is to see if the spiritual concept of six ministries can have a practical application in assisting a congregation to shape its worship space. Can the six ministries invoke Plans that will do this?

To prove this I am quoting six examples of existing churches which embody these principles. These examples are taken from my book[29] *Rebuilding the Church on a New Foundation* where I list twenty-four examples of churches built with the Six Plans. The purpose of that listing with so many examples is to reassure a congregation that such churches can be quite ordinary, while the purpose of my listings here is to show that churches with such qualities are possible. (If I wanted to prove white swans are normal I would need to study a thousand birds, but to prove that black swans may exist a single example would be sufficient.) So here follow six examples which show how six churches, each configured to one of the Six Plans, has integrated one of the six ministries into its worship. The six ministries are:

- Contemplation, the Ministry supported by the First Plan.

- Pastoral Care, the Ministry supported by the Second Plan.

- Witness, the Ministry supported by the Third Plan.

- Dedication, the Ministry supported by the Fourth Plan.

- Evangelism, the Ministry supported by the Fifth Plan.

- Justice, the Ministry supported by the Sixth Plan.

---

29. Robinson, *Rebuilding the Church on a New Foundation*.

SACRED JOURNEY
Support for Contemplation
Testing the First Plan

The table is in the center of the space.

The worshipers gather around it.

The children, and the very old, those especially loved, are in the front.

Candles on the table light the faces of all around,

they focus their attention on the Feast.

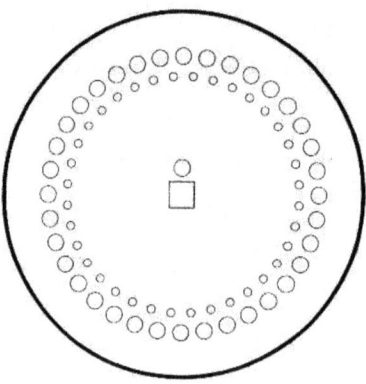

FIGURE 48. The First Plan, for the ministry of Contemplation.

The inward focus is directed towards the center, away from the walls. The walls that surround this space have no decoration or embellishment. They arch over the space to form a dome, white and featureless. The dome surrounds the space, contains it, and keeps it safe. The dome is not disturbed by chaos and hostility outside. It creates a totally internal serenity.

The Test
St. Mark's Catholic Church, Burlington, Vermont
Freeman, French, and Freeman, Architects, 1944

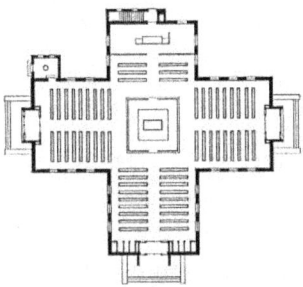

FIGURE 49. Plan of St. Mark's Church, Burlington, VT; showing the central placement of the altar.

EZRA STOLLER ESTO PHOTO

FIGURE 50. In the foursquare St. Mark's Catholic Church the worshipers are gathered in a ring around the altar.

St. Mark's Catholic Church was built out of a willingness to re-examine the traditions of the Mass: to retain what is eternal and to be prepared to change that which is not. This was in the 1940's, twenty years before Vatican II blew a breath of fresh air through the Catholic Church.

In those days most catholic altars were built up against the end wall of the church, and the priest celebrating Mass had his back to the people. The people could not see what he was doing; they had to take it on faith. Father Tennien of St. Mark's Church saw no reason why the people could not have a more involving role in the Mass, and he proposed the radical step of bringing the altar into the center of the church.

The people sit in a ring around the altar, a square ring rather than a round one, but a ring nevertheless, and they witness the Mass from three sides. The architects contained this seating arrangement in three rectangular volumes, and by adding a fourth for the choir and sacristy they created within a traditional cruciform plan an innovative arrangement for worship.

Support for Pastoral Care
Testing the Second Plan

The people remember the world.

In the sanctuary the people have separated themselves from the world

but they are the same people that have been shaped by the world.

The people seek peace while remembering conflict.

They seek healing, while remembering pain.

They seek faith, while remembering fear.

The Second Plan accepts this duality:

the duality of the Perfection of Christ and the cares, afflictions and fears of the people.

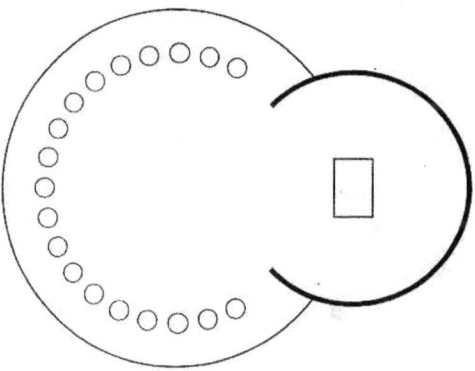

FIGURE 51. The Second Plan, for the ministry of Pastoral Care.

The walls are formed in the shape of two circular arcs, or two intersecting domes. The smaller dome surrounds the altar. The candles on the altar illuminate it, brilliantly. Its walls are strong, without openings. They withstand the world and preserve a heavenly peace. The people gather in the larger dome. The walls of this dome do not have to be so strong. They do not have to withstand the world. The people are not afraid of the world, or rather, they have the courage to bring their worldly fears with them when they come to worship. They gather as whole persons with all their humanity, their sexuality, their creativity. Light from the chalice spills out over them, a light not from the world but from the Holy Spirit.

The essential features of the Second Plan are:

>Strong walls to preserve the safety of the space.

>Permeable walls to allow the people to enter;

and, most importantly,

>Free access between the People and the Sacraments.

TESTING THE SECOND PLAN
Chapel in the Cardinal Flahiff Basilian Centre, Toronto
Ernest Cormier, Architect, 1949 / Fr. Robert Madden CSB, 1977

The walls of this chapel are strong and protective, and at the same time offer easy access. The strength is obvious—the walls are faced with stone, and although there are windows these are set high in the walls so nobody can look in from outside, and they are glazed with an Art-Deco composition of milky glass with brightly colored accents.

Access needs a bit more explanation. The chapel is attached to the Cardinal Flahiff Basilian Center, a three-story residence for retired priests, and each floor connects with the chapel. A corridor on the second floor of the residence building connects with the choir loft located over the narthex. The third floor of the residence, an infirmary for those older fathers who require nursing care, has a smaller balcony which overlooks the chapel and can be seen at a high level in the photograph of the interior of the chapel. By opening the doors to the balcony the sound of the Mass being sung can be heard by the residents of the nursing floor, so access to the space is achieved on many levels.

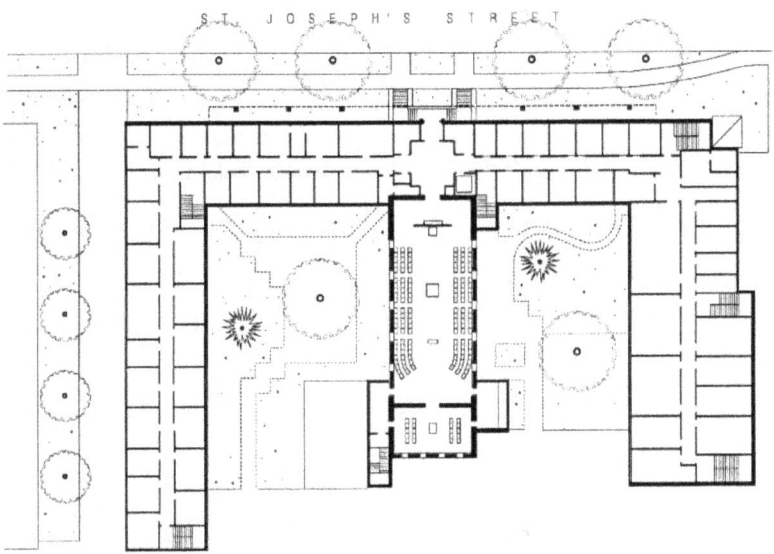

FIGURE 52. Main floor plan of the Cardinal Flahiff Basilian Center.

FIGURE 53. The Art-Deco interior of St. Basil's Chapel, with a central altar, is accessed on three levels.

The most important requirement for the Second Plan is that there should be no impediment or barrier between the People and the Sacrament. Some of the community are seated a mere six feet from the altar, and this physical closeness symbolizes for us the spiritual closeness we all experience.

Support for Witness
Testing the Third Plan

The dome is breached.

The light shines out into the world.

The People and Christ are together.

They look out into a world created by God's will,

and shaped by man's will.

Inside: the people see the world.

Outside: the world sees the light of the people at prayer.

The Third Plan is the Plan of Witness,

the plan that proclaims Christ's presence in God's world.

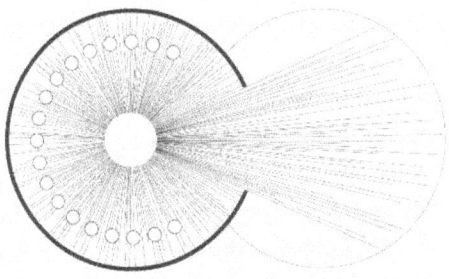

FIGURE 54. The Third Plan, for the ministry of Witness.

SACRED JOURNEY

The dome is pierced and the people see the world. The world into which they were born, the world where they work, the world which is their home. They see the world but they do not go out into it. The people gather round the altar. The light of the altar shines over the people and out into the world. The world sees the light and the world sees the people at prayer. The people at prayer and the light of the Eucharist are the witness of Christ's presence in the world. The Third Plan is the Plan of Witness.

Testing the Third Plan
St. Peter's Lutheran Church, New York City
Hugh Stubbins and Associates, Architects, 1976

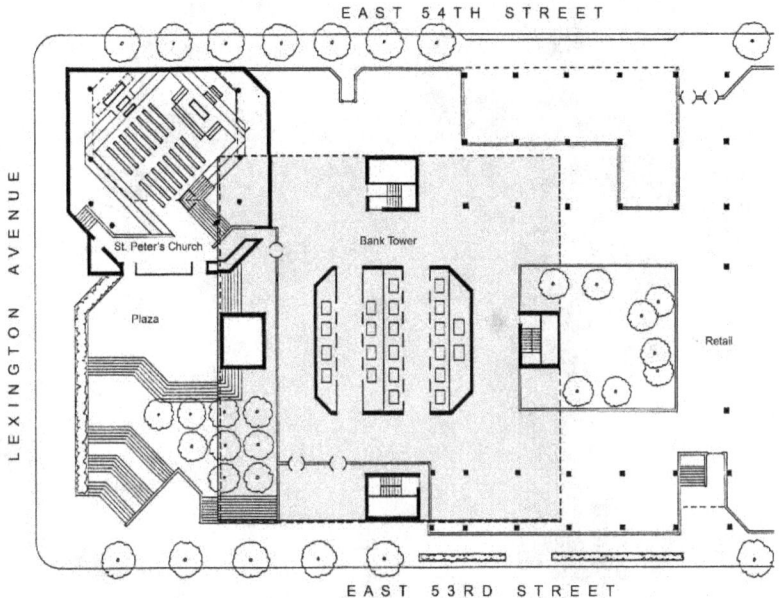

Figure 55. Plan of St. Peter's Lutheran Church in the northwest corner of the Citicorp Center, Lexington Avenue, New York City.

St. Peter's Church on Lexington Avenue at 54th Street in downtown Manhattan presents with great clarity an example of the working out of the Third Plan. The archetypal Third Plan is a breached dome. The dome was selected to symbolize the impenetrable quality of the walls.

FIGURE 56. Work and worship are seen together in St. Peter's Lutheran Church. Everything is movable except the organ and the font.

This does not mean that the building has to be shaped like a dome: rather, it is a way of saying that for the Third Plan the space inside must be secure. In St. Peter's the sanctuary is at basement level, and this gives us strong walls and a safe space.

Testing the Third Plan

Although the church is at basement level a lantern in the roof of the church projects through the main floor where a breach in the dome is a way for the worshiping people to see the world, and a way for the light of the Eucharist to be witnessed by the world. Windows in this lantern look down into the church beneath, so the casual passer-by on the sidewalk might be surprised to see below him a congregation at prayer. The passer-by might also see a concert, a lecture, a jazz festival, a folk mass, or just a quiet place to be. The public has responded to this with enthusiasm. St. Peter's Lutheran Church in Citicorp Center must be considered one of America's most successful urban churches.

The tall window over the altar reveals to the congregation the office towers across the street on Lexington Avenue, as well as a passing Lexington Avenue bus. Thus the worshipers can see, in the same glance, the altar where they worship and the offices where they work. World and worship are brought together.

Support for Dedication
Testing the Fourth Plan

Work needs to be done in the world.

The worshipers have found a new security in a common purpose.

They no longer need the security provided by the enclosing dome.

They are on a march,

a pilgrimage,

a sacred journey.

The people have been drawn together by the Eucharist.

This gave them strength.

Now they are moving into a new place, with new challenges.

The people all face the same direction. They do not need to face one another because they knew they had become a community the moment they committed themselves to their journey. Even though they do not face one another, they are in fact physically close to one another. They are held together by a common faith, and embarked together on a Sacred Journey. Their needs are few. They travel light. Their worship takes place on the road.

The essential features of the Fourth Plan are the linear quality of the space; and, most importantly, an endless pathway extending beyond the confines of the space.

The Fourth Plan is unlike all the other plans. It has a strong linear quality, to represent the Way. The Way is roofed, a vault arches over the roadway from one side to the other. This vault is not dark and heavy.

Testing the Fourth Plan

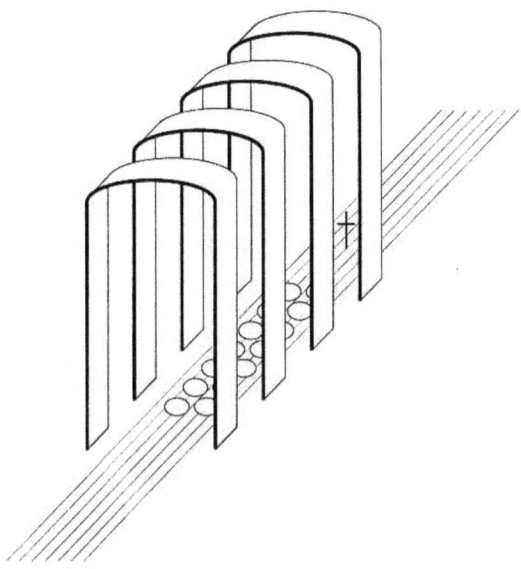

FIGURE 57. The Fourth Plan, for the ministry of Dedication.

Its purpose is not to withstand forces pressing in on the Way. In fact, it is good if it can admit daylight, so the people do not feel they have entered a cave. If the vault is built of alternately clear and solid sections, those moving through the space will experience alternate light and darkness, their lives measured out in nights and days.

The Fourth Plan is supportive of those who are brought together for a short time for a common purpose, and who know that later they must separate. It works well for the worship of schools and universities, where the goal is to equip oneself for a life in the world beyond. The Fourth Plan is also supportive of the worship of the business community, those whose labor in the World supports the worship of the People in an act of dedication.

We all have something to learn from this Plan because a journey continually confronts us with something new. The Fourth Plan is the plan of Dedication.

Sacred Journey
Trinity College Chapel, University of Toronto
Sir Giles Gilbert Scott, Architect, 1953

Scott's greatest work, and one of the twelve most beautiful buildings in North America. Most of Scott's works were in a heavy-handed and ponderous Gothic: here Gothic is interpreted with grace and lightness.

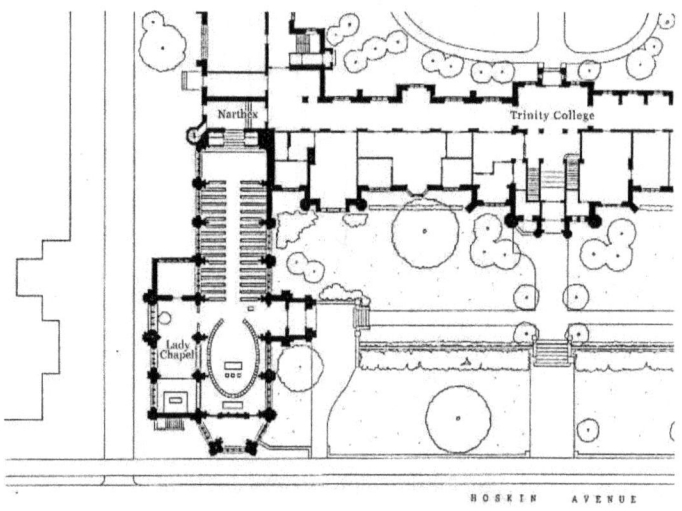

FIGURE 58. Plan of Trinity College at the University of Toronto.

This chapel fulfills, precisely, all the requirements for the Fourth Plan. The entrance and narthex are at an upper level. A wide flight of steps descends into the chapel. It is like coming down from a mountain and entering a valley. Valleys are linear, a place to journey, as opposed to mountain tops which are discrete places from which to see the view. At the moment of entering the chapel, as we stand at the top of the steps, we see our whole journey laid out before us. The chapel is very long, very high, and very narrow. The form of the space bespeaks journey. The walls are in pale tones of grey with repetitive pilasters to mark our progress on our way, but nothing is so arresting as to cause us to stop. The chancel is marked by a single step. The point at which the chapel ends is left ambiguous, as Sacred Journey is not to be confused with arrivals. As the table altar is relatively transparent the high altar can be seen through its open framework. The high altar is relatively heavy, but it is of the same stone as the screen in front of

FIGURE 59. The Chapel of Trinity College, Toronto, showing how The Way extends to the chancel, to the pierced altar screen, through the apse, and beyond.

which it stands, and into which it merges. The screen itself is pierced with openings through which we can see the apse. The apse has much glass, but it is a clear figured glass which permits light to pass but obscures vision.

So we are left with no clear statement as to where the space ends—is it at the altar, the screen, the apse, the window, or outside? Wherever we look, the end is elsewhere. This carefully-wrought ambiguity, by refusing to end the space at a definite point, allows the linear quality of Sacred Journey to extend beyond our vision. This is evidence of a master at work.

The final felicity is that the chapel serves a university community. We know we will be together for just a short while as we journey together for a common purpose. Soon we will graduate, separate, and form new relationships in new places. But while we are together we have the Eucharist as our strength and journeying together as our purpose.

Support for Evangelism
Testing the Fifth Plan

A space opens to those on the journey.

The travelers are welcomed.

The walls of the Fifth Plan are open,

offering shelter to those on the journey,

a sacred journey to which they will return,

gathering others with them on the Way.

The walls of the space curve round in a parabola, enclosing and protecting the altar. The lights on the altar reflect from these walls and form a beam of light shining down the path the pilgrims are taking.

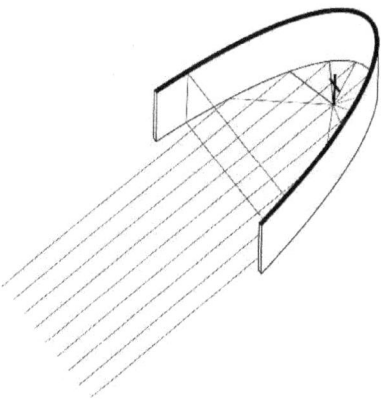

FIGURE 60. The Fifth Plan for the ministry of Evangelism.

The end wall of the space is transparent, so the people can see the lights when they are yet far off. Guided by the light, the people enter the space and gather round the altar. As they share in the sacraments they forge themselves into a community. When they have received the sacraments and they turn around to return to their places they see how the lights from the altar continue to shine out from the building and become the Way. As the people take this shining path out into the world they again become individuals, where they meet and greet other wanderers and invite them too to return with them and share in the feast.

In the Fifth Plan the voyagers find a safe harbor, not a permanent berth. The parabolic form of the space implies movements both inwards and outward. It accepts the travelers, nurtures them, and sets them on their way. This form of space is appropriate for those whose focus is evangelism. The people move out into the world to share the good news and bring the World to the Sacrament, inviting them to come back to meet, join and work with the community.

Testing the Fifth Plan
Die Heilig Kreuz Kirche, Bottrop, Ruhr, Germany
Rudolf Schwarz, Architect, 1952–57

The Fifth Plan receives, blesses and releases. It is the home church for missionaries, teachers and greeters, those who take seriously Christ's instruction to grow the church. Without wallet and staff they are out on the Way, guiding and welcoming. We are delighted when they spend some time with us, and yet we know their work is elsewhere.

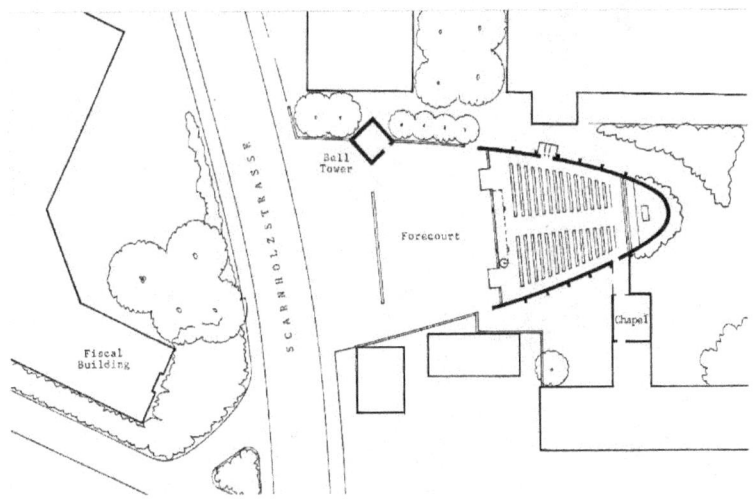

FIGURE 61. Plan of Die Heilig Kreuz Kirche in Bottrop, Germany.

The essential feature of the Fifth Plan is the easy coming-and-going of the people. This is the plan that welcomes pilgrims and sends them on their way. In Bottrop the welcome is expressed by the glazed entrance screen which expresses the open-ness of the interior to those still outside. The screen bears a huge spiral pattern of stained glass, which is even more impressive from within. This, together with the extending wing-walls, illustrates a church reaching out into the secular world, reaching out as Christ reaches out to humanity. This welcoming of the World to the Sacrament is the fundamental relationship of the Fifth Plan. The interior is impressive in its simplicity which extends to the church furnishings and appointments and creates an interior of clarity, austerity, and security. The congregation finds itself in a

FIGURE 62. An interior of great strength, calm, and integrity.

condition of dynamic tension between the Sacrament and the World, between being welcomed and being dismissed.

The Lord extends his arms in welcome to his dear people, and then he charges them to return to the world to bring in more souls. He offers them the holy gifts, and when they have received them and they turn to leave they turn to once again face their World.

Support for Justice
Testing the Sixth Plan

*The people, in a dome of light, gather round the altar,
but their attention is directed outwards towards the world.*

The work of the people is healing the world.

In this they will be scattered through the world, like seeds.

The dome is transparent.

The people can see the world all around them.

The dome focuses their vision.

In the center of the dome is the altar.

*Light from the altar shines on the people, illuminates their hearts,
and continues to shine out past them into the world.*

*The people see a world illuminated by the light from the altar,
a light that shines within them.*

*When the people go into the world they take the light of the Eucharist into
the world with them.*

*The world only distantly sees the light from the altar,
but the world experiences the light in the hearts of the people.*

*It is this Light which the people take out into the world
that can heal the world.*

The Sixth Plan is appropriate for those seeking change in the world. It is for congregations devoted to support for the environment, care for the suffering, right government for the nation, corporate responsibility, and a just society. It is the plan for those that wrestle with the forces of privilege, prejudice, and oppression. The Sixth Plan is the plan for Justice. It is the plan for those who struggle to create a world worthy for the coming of Christ.

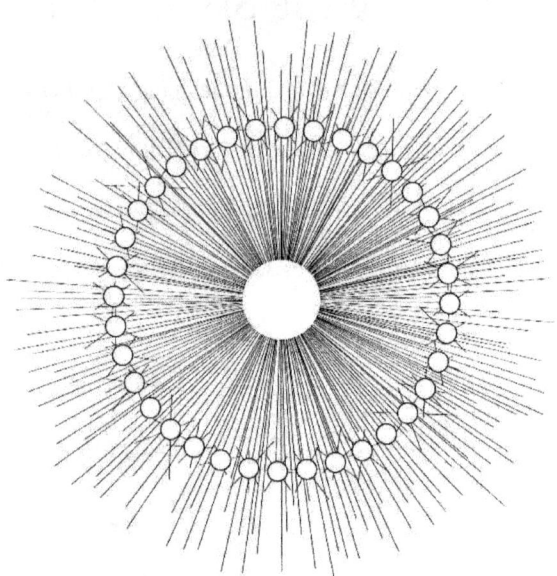

FIGURE 63. The Sixth Plan, for the ministry of Justice.

This Plan may exist in many forms. Ideally it is a dome of glass, so the light of worship can shine in all directions. It could be a completely open structure, or a structure with openings all around the perimeter, to permit the people carrying the light to go forth into all the world as an expression of the relationship of the parameters for the ministry of Justice, where the People go out into the World to bring forth justice and freedom and peace for all God's creatures.

TESTING THE SIXTH PLAN
Salvation Army Meeting, KwaMashu, Natal, South Africa

FIGURE 64. The open-ness of the Sixth Plan is demonstrated at a Salvation Army meeting in South Africa.

In South Africa, during the regime of apartheid, KwaMashu, like all black townships, was a center of unrest. The townships would be located in the next valley, round the bend of the river, on the other side of the hill. The citizens of Durban have heard of KwaMashu, in fact they have heard a lot about it, but they have never visited it. For the most part they have no direct experience of its existence. This is a Light that they do not see directly. A reflection of this light has to be carried out to them, in the heart.

Passing the Test

So there we have it. It will have to do for now; but this Test too will pass. The Gothic church had to pass the Medieval Test, the Victorian church had to pass the nineteenth century Test, so this Test too, although eternal in its form, will pass. It will not last forever.

It has taken Rudolf and myself almost a hundred years to craft this Test; so its "best-before" date could be in the foreseeable future. Once again we will have to go back to the early church so a new church can grow again as new—but the early church itself was as divided as this one is, and perhaps what survived was not the most deserving. Perhaps we will need to go back even further, back to the stable.

Epilogue

Our pilgrimage is completed, but our journey continues. This will be a sacred journey; and on it we wish you well

We were companions for Brother Rudolf even though we were separated by fifty years, by an ocean, and by a language.

His journey was much more difficult than ours. He had to strike out through rough country, not being sure of where he was heading, while we had a map.

As it happens, things are working out perfectly. If, in a parallel universe, Rudolf and I could have been companions charged with creating a single book, only one of us would have prevailed. Either I would have pruned his flowering tree to leave but a single bare branch, or he would have allowed his seeds to float away in the wind, never reaching the earth where they could be planted and take root.

Our pilgrimage is over, and now our work begins, but perhaps we should not be so seriously self-important about it. To give Schwarz the last word (68, line 24): "But in the end God is utterly different. And while the ascetic is scaling the lonely peaks perhaps God is in the valley, playing with the children and the flowers."

Toronto, 2020

Bibliography

Andrae, Johann Valentin. *The Chemical Wedding of Christian Rosencreutz*. Strassburg: Zetzner, 1616.

St. Augustine of Hippo. *City of God*. Translated by Henry Bettenson. London: Penguin Books,1972.

Barthes, Roland. *The Responsibility of Forms*. New York: Hill and Wang, 1985.

Brown, Dan. *Angels and Demons*. New York: Pocket Books, 2000.

Claudel, Paul. *Le Soulier de Satin*. (prologue to Act One)

Cyril of Jerusalem. *Mystagogical Catechesis*, II.4.

Donne, John. *The Sunne Rising*, 1633.

Evans-Wentz, Walter. *The Tibetan Book of the Dead*. London: Oxford University, 1927.

Goethe, J. W. von. "Die Hände wollen sehen, die Augen streicheln" quoted in Juhani Pallasmaa. *The Eyes of the Skin*. UK: Wiley Academy, 2005.

Guardini, Romano. Zum Geleit: *Vom Bau der Kirche*. Heidelberg: Verlag Lambert Schneider, 1938.

———. Zum Geleit. Translated by Gerald Robinson. See Foreword.

Harris, Cynthia. "Translator's Invitation" in Schwarz: *The Church Incarnate*, 1958.

Hone, William. *The Apocryphal New Testament, being all the Gospels and other Pieces now extant, attributed in the first four centuries to Jesus Christ, his Apostles, and their Companions, and not included in the New Testament by its Compilers*. London: William Reeves, 1820.

Hughes, Gerard W. *In Search of a Way*. Sydney, Australia: E.J. Dwyer Publishers, 1978.

Michell, John. *City of Revelation*. New York: Ballantine Books, 1972.

Reid, Robert L. *Commentary on the Documents of Vatican II*. Edited by Herbert Vorgrimler. New York: Herder and Herder, 1967.

Robinson, Gerald. "Liturgical Architecture: Creating Space for Worship." *Toronto Journal of Theology* 28/1, 2012, University of Toronto Press, 2012.

———. *Rebuilding the Church on a New Foundation*. Eugene, OR: Wipf & Stock, 2020.

Schwarz, Rudolf. *The Church Incarnate*. Translated by Cynthia Harris. Chicago: Henry Regnery, 1958

———. *Vom Bau der Kirche*. Heidelberg: Verlag Lambert Schneider, 1938.

Spencer-Brown, G. *Laws of Form*. London: George Allen & Unwin, 1969.

The Talmud, *Berakhot 6*.

Wotton, Sir Henry. *The Elements of Architecture, 1624*

Photo Credits

1. Henry Regnery Company, *The Church Incarnate,* 1958.

7. David Lown, Rome.

8. Staatsgalerie Stuttgart

9, 14, 15, 26, 27, 45, 59. Author

13. Photo Collection of the Kalmbach Publishing Company.

15, 31. Michael Robinson, London.

17. Carlos Celis Cepero, Caracas. Venezuela.

32. *Notes on the Cathedrals*, vol 1. London: SPCK 1904.

38. Wiki Commons

50. Ezra Stoller/ESTO Photo.

53. David Pereya.

56. Norman McGrath Photographer.

62. Cristoph Pfau / Der Oberstadtdirektor Stadt Bottrop, Germany.

64. The Salvation Army Canada and Bermuda Territory, *The War Cry.*

Index to Cross References

Topics identified by page and line number in *The Church Incarnate*, are here related to pages where they are referred to in this text.

The Foundation
3/ 9   11
3/16   15
6/16   54
7/29   13
8/11   13
9/26   13
11/27   14
12/ 1   67
15/10   17
19/15   18
22/32   21
24/12   18
27/ 3   18
27/ 5   21
27/12   19
27/21   21
31/ 9   19
31/ 9   84

The First Plan
36/ 1   31
38/10   33
65/ 9   35

The Second Plan
68/24   117
77/21   36
78/ 2   60
88/24   66
89/ 6   60

The Third Plan
95/ 3   22
101/ 7 47
103/11 53

The Fourth Plan
114/13 55
115/ 1 55
115/ 6 57

139/ 5 64
140/ 7 65
148/ 1 58
150/23 60
153/14 65
154/ 3 22
176/15 68
178/ 9 68

The Fifth Plan
160/ 6 69
176/15 70
178/ 9 69

The Sixth Plan
180/14 73
182/15 73

The Seventh Plan
190/ 4 83
191/15 80
191/29 80
193/31 80
193/ 7 82
197/27 71
205/ 9 12

The Test
211/ 3 86
212/15 88
212/31 88
213/28 89
216/ 1 87
224/13 87
227/11 85
227/16 59
227/23 22
228/24 88
229/14 89
231/18 90

Index

A

altar, 5, 11, 32–36, 43, 49, 55, 60–63, 66-69, 92, 94, 97-102, 105-108
ambiguity, 107
Apocrypha, The, 8, 86
Architect/Builder, 11, 43, 59, 88–91
atonement, 10
Augustine of Hippo, 27

B

Barnabas, Epistle of, 8, 86
Barthes, Roland, 84
Body of Christ, 5, 10–13, 17, 21, 34
Bottrop, Germany, 22, 70, 110

C

Caracas, Venezuela, 24
Cathedral of All Times, 78–80
chalices, 22, 95
chancel, 5, 7, 105
Church Incarnate, The, 2, 14, 86
Churches
    Basilica Pius X, Lourdes, 18, 20
    Flahiff Basilian Centre, 96
    Heilig Kreuz, Bottrop, 22, 70
    Holy Trinity, Stratford, 6
    Mary Chapel, Glastonbury, 33
    Orthodox Communion, 12, 22, 44
    Salvation Army, S. Africa, 114
    Santa Sabina, Rome, 7, 12
    St. Fronleichnam, Aachen, 60
    St. Mark's, Burlington VT, 95
    St. Peter's, Manhattan, 100
    St. Peter's, Rome, 43
    Trinity College Chapel, 105
    Whitby Abbey, 7

City of God, 27
Claudel, Paul, 3
communion table, 11, 43
congregation, 5, 7, 22, 26, 33, 45, 54, 74, 88, 90
Contemplation, Ministry of, 28-35, 39, 51, 85' 91-93
Creation, 25-27, 77
crossing, 5, 12
crucifixion, 7–12
Cycle of Plans, 72, 81
Cycle of Worship 26, 30, 52-54, 72- 74, 81,
Cyril of Jerusalem, 48

D

Dark Chalice, 3, 67
Dedication, Ministry of,29,, 55-65, 103–107
doctrine, 12, 32, 59, 68, 82, 87
dome, 32-38, 44, 47-57, 73. 91-95, 112-113
Donne, John, 15

E

Eastern rite—see Orthodox
Eilers, Fr. Wilhelm, 70
El Silencio, 24-25
Epistle of Barnabas, 8, 88
Evangelism, Ministry of, 29, 66-71, 106-111
eye, The. 14–18, 38, 48, 71, 75

F

Fifth Plan, The, 4, 66-71, 90, 108-111
First Plan, The, 31-35, 36, 37, 39, 45, 72-73, 77, 82, 90, 91-93

Fourth Plan, The, 55-64, 65-66, 69, 90, 103-107

G

gematria, 8-9
God, 12-14, 17, 27, 33–36, 38–39, 42-46, 55–64, 72, 79-83
Grand Central Terminal, 20
Guardini, Romano, *ix*, 2, 5, 79

H

hand, The, 14, 18, 75
Harris, Cynthia, 2, 3, 14
heart, 5, 34, 75, 112-114

I

icons, 12, 13, 22
iconostasis, 23, 44, 45

J

Justice, Ministry of, 28, 29, 72, 73, 90, 112-114

K

Kettle, John, 2
KwaMashu, South Africa, 114

L

Lao Tzu, 84
Laws of Form, 79
Light, 14-18, 21. 42, 46–49, 53-54, 69, 71, 73, 75, 99, 113, 114
Liturgical Consultant, 84

M

Mantilla-Bazo, Victor, 26
Mataré, Ewald, 71
Mies van der Rohe, Ludwig, 2
ministries–see Six Ministries

models, 21–23, 31, 57, 72-79, 87
modern architecture, 21
Multscher, Hans, 10

N

nave, 5

O

Orthodox Communion, 12, 22, 44

P

parabola, 4, 70, 109
parameters of worship, 27, 36, 45, 53. 62, 67, 74, 81
Pastoral Care, Ministry of, 29, 36-39, 53, 55, 92, 94-97
perfect numbers, 26
pews, 60, 71
Philip, St., 32
pilgrimage, 56, 64, 66-71, 103, 117
Plans: see Six Plans
processions, 3, 58, 63–65

Q

quantum universe, 15

R

Rebuilding the Church, 26, 31, 90
reincarnation, 84
Responsibility of Forms, 86
Robinson, Gerald, 18, 26, 90
Royal Ontario Museum, 76

S

Sacred Meeting, 38
Sacred Parting, 39, 46
Second Plan, The, 36-39, 44. 45, 55, 90, 94-97
Seventh? Plan, The, 76-80
Shaping Space for Worship, 14

Sixth Plan, The, 66-71, 90, 108-111
Six Ministries:
   Contemplation, Ministry of, 8, 28–33, 51, 85, 91–93
   Pastoral Care, Ministry of, 29, 36-30, 52, 53, 94-97
   Witness, Ministry of, 29, 46 49-54, 93, 98-102
   Dedication, Ministry of,29,, 55-65, 103–107
   Evangelism, Ministry of, 29, 66-71, 106-111
   Justice, Ministry of, 29, 30, 75, 77, 92, 113, 114
Six Plans:
   The First Plan, 23, 26, 32-40, 46, 76, 84, 92, 93
   The Second Plan, 36-39, 44. 45, 55, 90, 94-97
   The Third Plan, 54-55, 69, 90, 98-102
   The Fourth Plan, 55-64, 65-66, 69, 90, 103-107
   The Fifth Plan, 4, 66-71, 90, 108-111
   The Sixth Plan, 72-75, 77, 82, 90, 112-114
Space, 5, 18-21, 23-25, 36-39, 44-47, 63, 65, 87
Spencer-Brown, G. 79

Steingruber, Johann, 23

T

Tao Te Ching, 84
Tau, letter, 8, 9, 10
tau cross, 8
Third Plan, The, 54-55, 69, 90. 98-102
Toronto City Hall, 41-43
Toronto Journal of Theology, 18
transepts, 5, 7, 10
Trinity College, 14, 105

V

Vatican II, 61, 93
Villanueva. Carlos Raul, 26
Vitruvius, 89
Vom Bau der Kirche, 1, 2, 23, 59, 71, 84, 86

W

weeping chancel, 6-7
Witness, Ministry of, 29, 46 49-54, 93, 98-102
worship, 12, 19, 25-35, 51, 66, 71-73, 81-85
worship space, 5, 11, 22, 34, 54, 81, 90
Wotton, Sir Henry, 89

www.ingramcontent.com/pod-product-compliance
Lightning Source LLC
Chambersburg PA
CBHW050836160426
43192CB00010B/2050